Gardening in Containers

BY ELVIN McDONALD

GROSSET
GOOD LIFE
BOOKS

PUBLISHERS • GROSSET & DUNLAP • NEW YORK

Acknowledgments

Cover photograph by Elvin McDonald

The author wishes to express his appreciation to the following for permission to use their illustrations in this book:

Aladdin Industries: p. 8 right, p. 22 top; Armstrong Nurseries: p. 86 middle top left; B E H Housewares Corporation: p. 13 top; Morley Baer: p. 30; Ralph Bailey: p. 44 bottom right; Bodger Seeds, Ltd.: p. 65; California Redwood Association: p. 9 top, p. 28 top, p. 28 bottom, p. 29 top, p. 29 bottom; Fred R. Dapprich: p. 50; Harold Davis: p. 6; Fleco Industries: p. 19 bottom; George W. Park Seed Co., Inc.: p. 32 top, p. 32 middle left, p. 32 middle right, p. 32 bottom, p. 33 top, p. 33 middle, p. 33 bottom, p. 46 top, p. 64; Howard Graff: p. 23, p. 42 middle; W. R. Grace & Co.: p. 88; The Greenhouse: p. 8 left; Hort-Pix: p. 10 top, p. 13 bottom, p. 42 bottom, p. 49 top right, p. 52 left, p. 52 right, p. 53 right, p. 60, p. 62, p. 68 top, p. 68 bottom, p. 70, p. 71 right; *House Beautiful:* p. 17 bottom; Jackson & Perkins: p. 7 left, p. 21 top, p. 21 bottom, p. 26 right, p. 48, p. 56; Leaf Fiberglass: p. 27 right, p. 49 bottom right, p. 51 top, p. 51 bottom; Ward Linton: p. 10 bottom left, p. 38, p. 42 top left, p. 44 top right, p. 46 middle; Lord & Burnham Greenhouses: p. 22 bottom; Elvin McDonald: p. 7 right, p. 10 bottom right, p. 16 top, p. 16 bottom, p. 18, p. 19 top, p. 20 bottom, p. 26 left, p. 27 left, p. 34, p. 35, p. 40, p. 41 top, p. 41 middle left, p. 41 middle right, p. 41 bottom, p. 42 top right, p. 45, p. 53 left, p. 63, p. 71 left, p. 85 top left, p. 85 top right, p. 85 middle top left, p. 85 middle top right, p. 85 middle bottom left, p. 85 middle bottom right, p. 85 bottom left, p. 85 bottom right, p. 86 top left, p. 86 top right, p. 86 middle top right, p. 86 middle bottom left, p. 86 middle bottom right, p. 86 bottom left, p. 86 bottom right; J. Horace McFarland Company: p. 46 bottom; Hamilton Mason: p. 44 top left; Arthur Norman Orans: p. 66; Pan-American Seed Company: p. 57 bottom; Maynard L. Parker: p. 9 bottom left, p. 12, p. 49 left, p. 54, p. 59; Paul J. Peart: p. 14 top, p. 44 bottom left; Peto Seed Company, Inc.: p. 57 top; Star Roses: p. 9 bottom right; Sturdi-Built Manufacturing Company: p. 24; Sutton & Sons Ltd.: p. 37; George R. Szanik: p. 14 bottom; Verilux TruBloom, Inc.: p. 20 top.

1976 PRINTING

Contents

1
The Movable Plants

Cleopatra did it on her barges. King Louis XIV did it at Versailles. But it is the modern-day Californians who have made container gardening our new national pastime, which may, depending on your personal interests, serve as a hobby, a sport, an avocation, or merely a pleasurable chore to make your surroundings more attractive.

Container gardening is many-sided. It is house plants and patio flowers and much more. The whole idea is based on having plants of all kinds and sizes whose roots grow in a mobile home. Mobility is the word. Indoors this means you can grow container plants where the indoor climate is to their liking, but for decorative effect you can move them around. Outdoors you can bring plants to the bud stage in a utilitarian nursery or growing-on area. When leafed out or flowering, wheel or carry them off to display at the front door or around your patio.

Besides mobility, climate is another important part of container gardening. Even in the coldest of up-North gardens you can enjoy tropicals outdoors while the weather is warm and bring them inside when cold or frost threatens. If you have a place indoors that is sunny and pleasantly warm and moist, many kinds can be kept in active growth all winter. For example, Chinese hibiscus and dwarf citrus will continue flowering. If you do not have sufficient good growing space indoors for all of your tropicals, you can maintain them in a kind of "hold" situation in any cool but frost-free place, like an unheated but light porch, until the arrival of warm weather the following summer. The key to success with this technique is to withhold all fertilizer and to keep the soil just barely moist while the plants are in a state of semidormancy.

OPPOSITE: Potted azaleas provide flowers on a patio.
ABOVE: Multicolored African violets on display stand.
RIGHT: Calamondin or dwarf orange flowers and
    fruits.

Influence of the African Violet

The major influence of California gardeners on container gardening in this country had a parallel development in the rest of the country that is still very much felt today. It is traceable to one single plant, the African violet or *Saintpaulia*. By the time the African Violet Society of America was founded shortly following the end of World War II, thousands of people were growing—or trying to grow in all sorts of conditions and places—the little plant with violetlike flowers from Usambara in what was then known as East Africa. By the 1950s African violets had become a major force popularizing indoor gardening, no longer a pastime of the wealthy alone. If someone's collection outgrew window space, the problem had an instant solution in fluorescent light. In fact, fluorescent light grew such flower-covered and perfectly symmetrical plants it immediately became apparent that in the competitions staged by the African Violet Society

it was unfair to judge plants grown in natural light with those from a fluorescent-light garden.

So the African violet paved the way for tremendous development in all that houseplants and indoor gardening represent. There was exploding interest and activity to justify the development of products designed specifically for growing better plants indoors, and dozens of single plant societies and gardening clubs sprang up.

It was not long before the roof garden, the patio, the terrace, the deck and the inside garden created special problems for plants that could be moved around, inside the house and out, in season and out.

Before you can enjoy container gardening, there are certain supplies you will want to acquire. Obviously, containers of one kind or another are necessities. These, whether to buy, build or find, are discussed throughout this book, according to the various kinds of plants and situations. Remember these general rules about pots and other containers: scrub and rinse them clean before using for planting; and when a plant outgrows a container, move it to the next size larger and immediately scrub and rinse clean the outgrown container. Then you can store it away or use it for another plant.

FAR LEFT: In space 2 by 4 feet a 3-level fluorescent-light stand provides 24 square feet of growing space.

LEFT: Mobility is the advantage of container gardening, here facilitated by a plant caddy.

ABOVE: Flowers, shrubs, and trees grow in redwood planters in this spacious outdoor living area.

BELOW: Grow containers of flowers in any convenient place, then wheel them to where you want blooms.

RIGHT: Could these be Cleopatra's potted roses?

ABOVE: Bushy young philodendrons fill this contemporary planter situated in bright light, but no direct sun.

LEFT: Potted succulents, marigolds, roses and geraniums bring flowers into this living area.

BELOW: Calathea (shown in color on the cover) thrives indoors in low-light areas; requires no direct sun.

2
What Do Plants in Movable Containers Need?

Psychologists tell us that having plants in our environment is vital to a healthy state of mind. In an earlier, more agrarian age, this was taken for granted. Now we have a much greater awareness of every individual's need for living with living plants. This appears to be universal. It has the power to bridge every communications gap known to the human race.

Adopting one plant whose roots are confined to a pot is the first step in getting back to nature. Especially a potted plant kept indoors, where you are solely responsible for providing it with all that makes a growing environment: light, temperature, moisture and food. Outdoors a potted plant may receive some natural moisture, but indoors you are totally responsible.

Becoming involved in container gardening is something every person can do. There is no such thing as a green thumb, a purple thumb, a brown thumb, or any other color thumb except skin-colored. Every person can grow plants. The only way to fail is not to try at all. No one who really tries can be the kiss of death to flora. Even if you've tried and failed, you have to be willing to try again.

Climate. Whether you want to grow a container plant in a clay pot, a Japanese jardiniere, or an elaborate planter box, as in a Florida room, indoors or outdoors, you must first evaluate the climate where that plant will grow. Climate is a word we tend to associate with vast geographical areas. We think of vacationing in or retiring to a "warm climate." On television we watch forecasters predicting the effects of widespread winter snowstorms and we think "cold climate." But actually we live indoors and outdoors in countless mini- or microclimates. To be aware of this is the first positive step toward becoming a successful gardener.

Light, Temperature, Humidity

Let's say you want to grow a pot plant on your desk—at work or at home. Before you can determine which plant is most likely to be

Arranging container plants in ever-changing displays is one of the great pleasures of gardening this way.

the right choice, think about the climate that exists on your desk. Make a checklist like this:

Light. Amount of light that reaches the surface of the desk at various times during the day. It may receive direct sun in the morning, during midday or in the afternoon. It may receive no direct sun at any time but bright daylight for several hours daily. Or it may receive no natural light at all, in which case a desk lamp may provide enough illumination to nurture a small-leaved English ivy or trailing philodendron. Full sun from an unshaded east- or west-facing window is usually referred to in most writings about house plants as *semisunny* or *semishady.* Full sun from an unshaded south-facing window translates to *sunny* or *semisunny.* Any bright exposure that receives no direct sun or only an hour or two, even a north-facing window, may be referred to as *semishady, shady,* or as bright indirect light.

Light evaluation is perhaps the most difficult part of determining the climate for a particular container plant. Generally speaking, if there is enough natural light by which to read or do needlework, there is enough light to grow certain plants that grow naturally in the shade. Throughout this book you will find discussions of various kinds of plants and with each a suggestion as to light requirement indoors or out. Since most plants are rather demonstrative about receiving too much light (leaves wilt and develop yellow, burned spots) or too little (leaves become pale, new stems are spindly and weak), don't be afraid to try a plant in questionable light. Just watch it, and if the plant's sign language indicates more or less light, try to accommodate it.

Temperature. This is much easier to evaluate than the amount of light. Generally speaking, if the temperature range is comfortable for you, it will also be comfortable for most container plants. There are exceptions, of course: tropicals that always want a toasty warm place or essentially cold-climate, outdoor plants that will survive indoors only in temperatures too chilly for human comfort. In books about houseplants or greenhouses, you will find the term *cool* used to describe a temperature range of approximately 40 to 60 degrees F. *Moderate* suggests a range of 55 to 70 degrees F. *Warm* represents average house temperatures, or a range of 62 to 75 degrees F. during that time of the year when artificial heating is required.

The greatest temperature problems have to do with too much heat. Cacti and other succulents from the dry, arid deserts of the world don't seem to mind drafts of artificial heat. Most leafy plants —Boston fern and asparagus-fern, for example—find it difficult to thrive directly over a radiator or other source of heat. Cacti and other succulents that grow wild in the jungle, as opposed to the desert—Christmas cactus and the *Epiphyllum,* or orchid cactus, for example— prefer moderate to warm temperatures with some moisture in the atmosphere instead of a hot, dry place.

Interestingly e n o u g h, many indoor plants do quite well with summer air-conditioning. In my office, in a sunny west window, I have many plants that thrive with the pots resting directly on the heating/air-conditioning unit. In winter warm air rustles the leaves all day long; in the summer it is a chilly breeze. One good rule of thumb to remember is that most container plants resent being at the same time either hot and dry or cold and dripping wet.

Humidity. Closely related to temperature is humidity, the amount of moisture in the air surrounding a container plant. Most indoor environments are painfully dry during that part of the year when artificial heat is required. In this day of fuel shortages and attendant high prices, it is amazing that public buildings continue to be overheated, and this holds

ABOVE: Small plants grouped together grow better. BELOW: Rex begonia enjoys humidity by bathroom sink.

ABOVE: *Fountain in indoor garden increases humidity.*
BELOW: *Lath shade for plants also helps cool bedroom.*

true of many homes as well. Excessive heat robs the air of all moisture and sets up a vicious cycle: the drier the atmosphere, the higher the temperature has to be for human comfort. In a lower temperature there tends to be more humidity —or at least it is easier to raise the humidity—and the result is greater human comfort and healthier plants.

Measuring the amount of humidity in a given space indoors is fairly simple if you invest in a hygrometer (available at hardware stores). This instrument will give you a readout in terms of the amount of humidity expressed in percentages from 0 to 100 percent. Anything up to 20 percent may be considered as *dry*; from 20 to 40 percent as *medium*; and from 40 percent up as *moist*.

Without a hygrometer it is fairly easy to determine if your indoor environment is *dry* because your respiratory system and dry skin will tell you. And, at the opposite, you can feel and smell a really *moist* atmosphere. It is in-between where evaluation is more difficult without an instrument to tell you.

If the soil in a pot is kept nicely moist at all times, most common houseplants will tolerate a dry atmosphere, but a *medium* amount of humidity is much more desirable, not only for plants but for the human occupants and fine wooden furniture as well, including the piano. It is almost impossible to have a medium amount of humidity indoors in artificial heat unless you use some kind of humidifier. If your home has a furnace, an automatic humidifier can be installed into that existing system. Otherwise, as in an apartment or office building, a portable humidifier will probably be the answer. For the treatment of respiratory illness, virtually every neighborhood drugstore and pharmacy sells room-size cool-vapor humidifiers that hold about two gallons of water. These vaporize up to four gallons of water in every 24 hours and thus require twice-a-day filling. There are also larger cool-vapor units sold for general humidification of several rooms in a dwelling. These hold about six gallons of water and need filling every two or three days.

Many times I sense a certain reluctance from individuals when I recommend the use of these humidifiers. I know they are thinking the atmosphere will smell dank and musty, but this is definitely not the case when the humidity is combined with some fresh air. In my own apartment the wintertime humidity ranges from 40 to 60 percent, combined with a little fresh air from windows kept open slightly even in cold weather. No one who has entered my apartment for the first time has ever complained of a musty, overly damp smell. Rather they comment on the lush greenery and the feeling of being revived by the pleasantly moist atmosphere.

Adding up your climate. Light, temperature, humidity: How much did you find on and around your desk—or whatever part of your environment where you want to grow plants? Once you have these facts firmly in mind, you can decide to find a plant uniquely suited to the environment you have, or you can alter that environment to fit the needs of a special plant you want to grow.

The rest of growing a plant in a clay pot or other handsome container indoors is relatively simple—you can provide and control water and nutrients in the soil or other growing medium simply by using common sense. If the surface soil feels dry to your fingers, give the plant a good drink of water. If it feels moist, additional water is probably not yet needed. If it is really wet, or if water is actually standing on the surface, check to be sure excess can drain properly. Very few container plants like to stand in water for more than an hour or two at a time.

Applying fertilizer to container plants is far less critical than watering. If you are growing in a medium based on real soil, earth—or dirt, as we used to say when I was a child—it will contain enough nutrients to sustain fairly good plant

growth with or without a precise program of supplementary feeding. However, if you are growing in one of the newer soilless mediums (based on a mixture of peat moss, perlite and vermiculite), regular feeding is a necessity. The possibilities of growing container plants in various soils or in a soil-less medium are discussed more fully in Chapter 13.

There are other factors involved in growing container plants. Bugs, for example. And diseases, though infrequently. And also plenty of other problems. To help you cope with these inevitabilities, I have prepared a chart of symptoms and what to do about them. This you will find also in Chapter 12.

Getting Started with Container Gardening

If you've never before tried growing a plant in a pot, or if you've tried and failed, some easy projects that require little or no investment of money can give results that are almost sure to build confidence.

Bean and pea gardens. Take a five- or six-inch flowerpot and fill it with potting soil, either from your garden or the kind you purchase in a bag wherever plants are sold. Add enough soil to the pot so that when you firm it down with your fingers the surface is one inch below the top of the pot. Take about six dried beans or peas (but not split peas) from your kitchen cupboard and scatter them over the surface soil. Cover them with about a half inch of potting soil; pat this down with your fingers. Add water until the entire pot of soil is moist. Place the pot in bright light or direct sun where temperatures would be comfortable for you. Within two or three days the seeds will begin to sprout. Add more water when the surface soil begins to feel dry as you pinch a little of it between your fingers.

This pot of beans or peas makes an

ABOVE: *Jeannene McDonald plants beans in pottery bowl.*

BELOW: *From avocado pit to tree takes about two years.*

almost instant garden of healthy green foliage. Children are often fascinated by this and can do it with some help. If you keep the pot always nicely moist in good light, the plants will grow well for several weeks, but since these are really for growing outdoors, don't expect too much of them. As soon as the growth ceases to be interesting and attractive, discard the plants. You can use the same pot of soil to grow another batch of peas or beans, or you can try something else. Incidentally, if you have a pet cat in your house, it may eat the bean or pea sprouts almost before the leaves have a chance to open.

Avocado tree or bush. Take the seed pit from a full-size ripe avocado. In clean water rinse off the seed, then dry it with a towel. Snuggle the bottom half, the larger part, of the pit about an inch deep into a pot of moist soil—perhaps the same you have used for a bean or pea sprout experimental garden described above. Keep the soil evenly moist at all times—not ever bone dry and not dripping with excess moisture for more than a few hours. When you see a sprout of growth, provide the young avocado with bright light and some direct sun shining on it if possible.

Once your avocado pit has sprouted, you have the beginnings of what can be a very fine houseplant that will last for as long as you like. If you want a bushy or shrublike plant, it will be necessary to pinch or cut out the top inch of tip growth after three or four leaves have opened out fully. This pinching or cutting will encourage two branches to grow where before there was only one. When these two branches each have three or four healthy leaves, again pinch or cut out the tip growth of each. Soon you will have one main stem, two secondary branches, and four growing points. Continue this pinching-branching-pinching procedure for as long as you have the plant.

If you want your avocado to form an

indoor tree with branches that spread out from a trunk, the procedure is slightly different in the early stages of growth. To form a single straight trunk, do not pinch out the main growing tip until you want branching to begin. If the avocado starts branching of its own accord, and some do, nip out any but the single strongest, hardiest, most vigorous growing tip. You may have to insert a sturdy bamboo stake in the pot and loosely tie the avocado stem to it, using half-inch-wide strips of plastic cut from a green garbage bag or plastic plant tie to do the tying. Once a trunk of sufficient height has grown, you can begin the pinching-branching-pinching routine the same as described for a bushy avocado plant.

Indoor avocados will adapt to various kinds of light, from shade (as in a north-facing window) to sun, but one thing they won't tolerate is being terribly hot and dry at the same time. This will cause all the older leaves to turn brown and crisp along the edges; some will have dry, dead areas within the leaves; and some leaves will die and drop off almost immediately.

Water gardening indoors. If you want to get into container gardening without so much as touching soil, you can grow cuttings in water. Take any clean glass vase or bottle and fill it with water. Ask friends who have container plants to give you some cuttings. Some good plants to root in water include wandering Jew, wax plant (*Hoya carnosa* and its varieties), trailing philodendron, English ivy, wax begonia, angel-wing begonia and Chinese evergreen (species or cultivar of *Aglaonema*). Before you put the cuttings in water, cut off any leaves from that part of the stem which will be submerged. The cuttings will form roots in water, and many will exist this way for weeks and months, if not years. For best results keep the containers filled with water, adding fresh from time to time. Once a month pour out all the old water, rinse

ABOVE: Coleus is an easy plant to grow in water.
BELOW: Hoya. Remove submerged leaves of stem in water.

out the container, then refill it with fresh water to which you have added a little houseplant fertilizer. To mix the fertilizer in water to the proper strength, read directions on the fertilizer box, then add fertilizer to water at one-fourth to one-fifth the strength recommended for feeding plants in soil. For example, if the label says to add one teaspoon fertilizer to one quart of water for soil, then add only one-fourth teaspoon of fertilizer to each quart of water you are going to use for your water-grown cuttings.

Experimenting with plants for containers. Beyond these suggestions for getting into container gardening without spending a lot of money or risking the loss of an established, purchased plant, you will find literally thousands of possibilities for container gardening indoors and outdoors. The photographs accompanying this chapter have been selected to give ideas for how to use and enjoy container gardens of all kinds. In subsequent chapters you will find photographs of specific plants along with guides telling precisely how to grow different kinds of plants in pots and other containers.

Once you get the feel for growing any plant in a container, indoors or outdoors, you will realize that almost anything is fair game. Even if a garden catalog or book says nothing about growing a particular plant in a container, don't be afraid to try. If you can provide the plant's requirements of light and temperature, then the rest is mostly a matter of giving the plant a container of sufficient size to support its root system, in combination with a thoughtful feeding and watering program. Half the fun is in the experimenting.

If you want containers of flowering plants outdoors in a shady place in the summer, then you'll grow impatiens at first because they're sure to perform well. Eventually, however, you'll begin to search the catalogs for other plants that flower in the shade because they'll make your garden more interesting.

It's the same indoors. If, for example, you want a beautiful foliage plant to grow in a corner where light is bright enough for you to read a name in the telephone book, but there is no direct sun, you might wisely select that Chinese evergreen, but in time you will want to experiment with other foliage plants to see if they will adapt to less than ideal lighting conditions.

Hybrid aglaonemas, forms of plain Chinese evergreen, are among the best plants to grow in low-light areas.

Indoor Gardens without Natural Light

If you have no light indoors sufficient to sustain plants, then some means of artificial illumination is the answer. Fluorescent light is the most efficient way to grow plants where natural light is not available. Ceiling fluorescents used for general illumination in most offices are too far away from plants to benefit much; they do supplement weak natural light. However, it is simple and fairly inexpensive to rig up a fluorescent unit specifically for growing plants. Here's how:

Take a standard industrial fixture that contains two 20-watt or two 40-watt tubes. Suspend it about 18 inches above a shelf or other surface on which you will place flowerpots. Ordinary fluorescent tubes may be used for growing plants, or you can invest in some of the special agricultural growth tubes such as Gro-Lux Wide Spectrum. One proven combination is to use one Cool White and one Warm White tube in each fixture. Burn the tubes 12 to 16 hours out of every 24; you'll find it more convenient to use an automatic timer so that day length is uniform regardless of your schedule and whether or not you're at home.

Where only leaf growth is desired, and no flowering plants are being cultivated, days of fluorescent light longer than 16 hours may be beneficial. In fact, in recent experiments I have done with leaf lettuce, 20-hour days of light—up to continuous illumination—have produced the makings of fresh-picked salads more quickly than with shorter daylight.

It is never necessary to combine incandescent light with fluorescent for growing plants. However, incandescent alone can be beneficial. In its simplest form this may mean a table or desk lamp burned 12 to 16 hours out of every 24, with a small plant or two placed within the range of brightest light. Small-leaved English ivies and trailing philodendrons do espe-

ABOVE: Sanseverias, top; bromeliads and small Norfolk Island pines, middle; two dracaena species, bottom.
BELOW: Blooming aphelandra (two zebras) and a jade plant.

cially well in this kind of illumination as do small terrariums planted with shade-loving plants.

More recently, indoor gardeners have discovered that certain kinds of incandescent floodlights can be used to supplement or to entirely replace natural light for maintaining and growing large foliage plants indoors. It is important to use floodlights, not spotlights. Spots concentrate the light so much that it tends to burn the foliage. Floodlights—for example, General Electric's Cool Beam and Sylvania's Cool-Lux—are available in sizes from 75 to 300 watts. Smaller ones can be placed in a range of 12 to 24 inches from the foliage; larger ones may need to be 24 to 36 inches away from the leaves. After a flood has been burning over a plant for about an hour, feel the leaves. If your fingers tell you that the leaf is warm, move the flood back or up another 12 inches. If an incandescent flood is a plant's sole source of light, burn it 12 to 16 hours out of every 24; if it is merely a supplement to some natural light, 6 to 8 hours daily will probably suffice. Floodlights for plant growth should be used in ceramic sockets. Suitable fixtures and stands are available from electrical and photographic supply houses, and also from lighting-fixture departments in some department stores. Ceiling track lighting systems offer an excellent means of housing floodlights for plant growth.

ABOVE: Fluorescent unit supplements light at dim window.
BELOW: Light unit and tray are suspended from ceiling.

Special Environments for Container Gardens

One of the easiest ways to be successful with plants indoors is to grow them in a special, glassed-in environment—a terrarium or bottle garden, for example. For greatest success with this kind of miniature garden, group plants together that share similar requirements—for example, kinds that need moisture and shade are especially suited to a bottle garden or closed terrarium. Kinds that need sun

ABOVE: Bubble bowl terrarium has a clear glass cover to keep plants inside in a moist atmosphere. A covered terrarium like this one needs bright reflected light, but if hot sun shines directly on it, temperatures inside will be too high for good growth. This kind of terrarium will grow to perfection in a bright north window or in a fluorescent-light garden. Keep outside of glass polished clean.

LEFT: To plant a terrarium, collect suitably small plants that require similar conditions for healthy growth. Here the choices for a terrarium that will be constantly humid and moist include small-leaved English ivy, a young Fluffy Ruffles fern, Dracaena sanderiana, dwarf palm, and rooted cuttings of mistletoe fig. The growing medium has been mounded into an interesting, naturalistic terrain.

ABOVE: Window greenhouse attaches like an air con-
ditioner.
BELOW: Standard window greenhouse with ventilator
top.

and more dryness—cacti and other succulents, for example—are better choices
for an open terrarium or dish garden.

One step beyond a terrarium or bottle
garden is the indoor planter, often built
along a glass wall section at floor level
or raised, just as they are outdoors.

Some homes have glassed-in gardens
beneath a skylight. You'll find these available by mail and at local garden centers.
The window greenhouse is a special pleasure for the container gardener. Some of
the smaller ones are installed in exactly
the same manner as a window air-conditioning unit. The larger window greenhouses are attached to the window frame
outdoors, or they can extend some inches
wider and higher than the dimensions of
the window, provided you have access to
all parts of the greenhouse by reaching
through the open window which the greenhouse covers.

Full-scale greenhouses are the dream of
nearly every person who gardens, and,
interestingly enough, to some who've never gardened at all but want to. If you are
serious in your desire to have a greenhouse, send away for the catalogs of manufacturers suggested in Appendix A. Prefabricated greenhouses continue to be one
of the best buys around. You'll find a
variety of architectural styles available
in sizes to suit almost any conceivable
situation. Many are designed in a modular
fashion so that you can add on units with
relative ease at a later date.

If the cost of heating a standard greenhouse worries you, consider building a
sun-heated pit. By this approach, solar
energy provides the heat at no cost to
you—or to our environment. The procedure is surprisingly simple. For example, if you want a sun-heated pit greenhouse 8 feet wide by 12 feet long, dig a
pit in the ground 4 to 5 feet deep and
slightly larger than the dimensions, siting
it from east to west. Add concrete or concrete block walls with a sill plate at the
top on which you will mount an A frame
with glass or plastic windows facing
toward the south and an insulated roof
wall facing the north. On cold nights and
cloudy, cold days, cover the glass or

ABOVE: *Home greenhouse opens into living area.*

This prefabricated lean-to greenhouse has glass to the ground, a feature that increases growing space and reduces construction costs. Often, heating can be provided by the dwelling's existing system.

plastic with heavy straw mats, old carpeting or sheets of lightweight plastic foam. These serve as insulation to keep the heat in and the cold out. On sunny winter days, remove the insulation materials as early as possible to allow maximum penetration of solar energy—which stores up heat against nighttime cold.

Built and managed as I have just described, a sun-heated pit greenhouse can be maintained in cold climates without any supplementary heat. Granted, in the dead of winter average temperatures may range only slightly above freezing to perhaps 50 degrees F., but in this environment it is still possible to grow an incredible variety of beautiful flowering plants—camellias, primroses, spring bulbs, azaleas and acacia, to name a few. By adding a little auxiliary heat, it is possible to run a sun-heated pit as a moderate-temperature greenhouse, and then you can grow anything save tropicals like philodendron, gloxinia and African violet. For example, in a moderate temperature range of nighttime lows between 45 and 55 degrees, and daytime temperatures perhaps edging up to 75 degrees on a sunny day, you can grow all kinds of geraniums, fragrant sweet-olive, winter sweet peas and pansies, and good crops of leaf lettuce, parsley, other herbs and flowering bulbs.

Besides studying the catalogs of greenhouse manufacturers, I would suggest also that you send 25¢ to the Superintendent of Documents, U.S. Government Printing Office, Washington, D.C. 20402, for a copy of Bulletin No. 357, "Building Hobby Greenhouses." For further reference I suggest also these publications:

Eaton, Jerome A., *Gardening Under Glass,* The Macmillan Company, 866 Third Ave., New York, N.Y. 10022.

Acme Engineering and Manufacturing Corp., *The Greenhouse Climate Control Handbook: Principles and Design Procedures,* Acme Engineering and Manufacturing Corp., Muskogee, Okla. 74401, $2.00.

Courtier, J. W., and Curtis, J. O., *A Simple Rigid Frame Greenhouse for Home Gardeners,* Cooperative Extension Service, Circular 880, University of Illinois, College of Agriculture, Urbana, Ill. 61801. Out of State, 10¢.

Courtier, J. W., and Curtis, J. O., *Home Greenhouses for Year-round Gardening Pleasure,* Cooperative Extension Service, Circular 879, University of Illinois, College of Agriculture, Urbana, Ill. 61801. Out of State, 10¢.

U.S. Department of Agriculture, *Plastic Covered Greenhouse Coldframe,* Miscellaneous Publication 1111, Washington, D.C. 20250.

3
Containers to Buy or Build

Containers for growing plants are all around us. You can buy clay or plastic flowerpots from thumb size to 20 inches in diameter—or larger. You can make do with household castoffs, for example, tin cans, cutoff milk cartons and gallon-size (or larger) plastic bottles. You can buy ready-made tubs and boxes of redwood or cypress (both moisture-resistant), or you can build your own planters using these woods, marine plywood or wood salvaged from shipping crates (which will not last more than a season or two unless you first treat the wood with a preservative). In the pages that follow, you will find photographs and diagrams depicting a number of handsome containers you can build for gardening indoors and outdoors.

What Size Container?

It's easy to fit plants to pots. For one thing, when you put a plant together with a pot, it should look right to your eye. You may be surprised to discover that what looks right to your eye, however inexperienced you may be as a gardener, will probably be right in a cultural sense. This has to do with esthetics which we learn by association and, for some persons, a natural sense of proportion and scale.

If you'd like a more precise guide, here is a general rule: For a plant that is growing mostly upright, the diameter of the pot should be one-third to one-half the height of the plant. By this rule of thumb a dieffenbachia (dumbcane) 18 inches tall needs a pot six to nine inches in diameter.

If the plant grows mostly in a horizontal plane, the same rule holds. For example, an African violet with a leaf span of nine inches will look right—and grow well—in a pot that measures from three to five inches across the top.

These two rules work fairly well for small or young plants. However, large bushes, trees and vines are not so easily defined. For example, a weeping fig tree six feet tall does not need a pot two to

Burro's-tail sedum in standard clay pot with saucer.

Climbing philodendron in woven terra-cotta pot.

three feet in diameter. It will do nicely in a pot or tub 12 to 14 inches in diameter and of about the same depth. Perhaps the general rule that can be applied here is that in addition to looking right to the eye, the container has to be large enough to balance the physical weight of the plant so that it stands firmly without danger of tipping over under average circumstances. For any large plant, whether it grows as a bush, a tree, a climbing or trailing vine, the container should also hold enough soil so that it is not constantly dry at the roots. If a container is too small, the soil will dry out so rapidly and so often that you will find it impossible to water often enough to sustain healthy root and leaf growth.

Although all of these rules are generalities and are to be taken as such, if you will consider them along with the visual sense you can develop just by studying all of the photographs in this book, you should have no problem either esthetically or culturally in fitting plants to suitable pots.

Clay or Plastic?

Both clay and plastic pots have advantages and disadvantages. Clay flowerpots are such classics in terms of design that they look right in virtually all settings—period, traditional or contemporary, elegant or casual. From a cultural viewpoint, unglazed clay pots have porous walls that transpire air and moisture. Consequently they dry out more rapidly than glazed pottery or plastic. Unglazed clay saucers seep enough moisture to damage wood floors and carpeting. To avoid this problem, cut a piece of half-inch cork to fit under each saucer. Excess

Young bird's-nest fern growing in white plastic pot.

Fiberglass cylinder pots and pedestal for plant display.

moisture evaporates through the cork, and under normal circumstances should never build up sufficiently to harm either carpeting or wood floors.

Glazed pottery containers and plastic pots require less watering than unglazed clay. The matching saucers are waterproof.

Containers without drainage holes require special attention to watering. Growing a plant successfully in a container without any drainage provision is not easy. A skilled workman may be able to drill a drainage hole for you in such a jardiniere. You can do it yourself in a metal container. I recommend planting in any utilitarian container that has drainage—even a tin can with holes punched in the bottom—and then slipping this inside of the decorative container that has no drainage. If you wish to plant directly in such a container, first add a good lay-er of pebbles, broken clay flowerpot or chipped charcoal, then proceed with planting. But whether you plant directly in a container without drainage, or indirectly by using a utilitarian liner, be cautious about applying too much water at any given time. If a container is to be used outdoors where rainfall reaches it, drainage is a necessity.

Glazed ceramic and plastic containers are easily kept clean in very much the same way you wash dishes. After prolonged use, a layer of mineral salts may build up along the edge or lip of the pot, and this should be removed by scrubbing with a soap pad or wire brush. Unglazed clay pots also build up this layer of mineral salts along the edges as well as the exterior walls. Again, all of this can be removed by scrubbing with a soap pad or wire brush and then rinsing in clear water.

Containers to Build

Severe demands are made on the wood from which a planter box is built. Direct contact with soil and periodic watering provide an ideal medium for decay and destructive insects. The use of redwood heartwood for planter-box construction will eliminate this problem. Redwood's preservatives are present throughout the heartwood. Therefore, minor surface checks and splits, which appear in all woods, will not affect redwood's interior resistance. These same conditions, which are ever present in planters, can lay open a surface-preserved wood's interior to insect and decay attack.

Redwood heartwood's durability is the result of a combination of chemical extractives which, occurring naturally, make applied preservatives unnecessary: every cell and fiber is naturally repellent to insects and decay-producing fungi.

Redwood is dimensionally stable. When kiln dried, it results in a lumber product that resists shrinking, swelling, checking and cupping. Dimensional stability means redwood planters will keep their shape despite extreme variations of moisture and temperature.

But it is probably redwood's beauty and versatility that have made redwood planters as popular as they are today. Redwood needs no finish. Weathering will turn the unfinished wood to an attractive driftwood gray—a pleasing backdrop for all flora. Or redwood may be finished with a variety of water repellents and light- or heavy-bodied stains to achieve almost any effect. And redwood's easy workability means it can be shaped to any specification.

All heartwood grades of redwood lumber are recommended for planters containing soil. These are *Clear All Heart,* for applications where a clear, knot-free wood is desired; *Select Heart* and *Construction Heart,* where knots are of little or no consequence. Containerized plant-

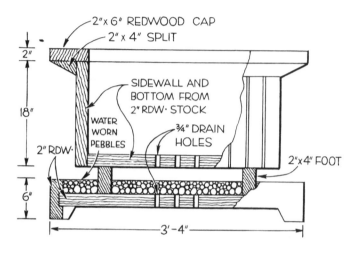

2" x 6" REDWOOD CAP
2" x 4" SPLIT
2"
18"
SIDEWALL AND BOTTOM FROM 2" RDW. STOCK
WATER WORN PEBBLES
¾" DRAIN HOLES
2" RDW.
6"
2"x4" FOOT
3'- 4"

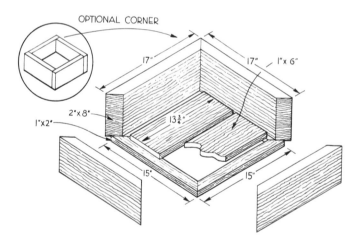

OPTIONAL CORNER
17"
17"
1" x 6"
2"x 8"
13¾"
1"x2"
15"
15"

ers used indoors may be constructed of heartwood or sapwood-containing grades.

Redwood heartwood's extractives can cause initial stains on concrete patios. To avoid this, the inside of the planter can be coated with a tar substance or lined with polyethylene film. A water repellent will discourage extractive staining, but allow two weeks before planting to let toxic agents become harmless. Another alternative is to set a new planter in a metal pan or similar container for the first two or three waterings to avoid stains.

Redwood planter boxes, whatever their design, require two preliminary precautions to make them maintenance-free. First, be sure to drill holes or leave narrow spaces between the bottom boards for water drainage necessary with any planter. Second, be sure that nails and metal fasteners are corrosion resistant. That is, the metal used in contact with redwood should be stainless steel, aluminum alloy or *top-quality,* hot-dipped galvanized. Otherwise, the chemical reaction that occurs when redwood extractives encounter iron and water will cause black streaks on the wood. More complete information on fasteners and finishes is available by writing the California Redwood Association, 617 Montgomery Street, San Francisco, California 94111.

Depending on your interests, you may wish at the same time to ask the California Redwood Association for any of a series of data sheets on garden uses of redwood. These include:

Building a Redwood Fence (3C2-2)
Building a Redwood Garden Shelter (3C2-3)
Redwood Garden Work Centers (3C2-4)
Redwood Deck Construction (3C2-5)
Patio Paving with Redwood (3C5-1)
Redwood Exterior Finishes (4B1-1)

Fir and other less expensive woods can also be used to construct containers, but they must be specially treated if they are to last.

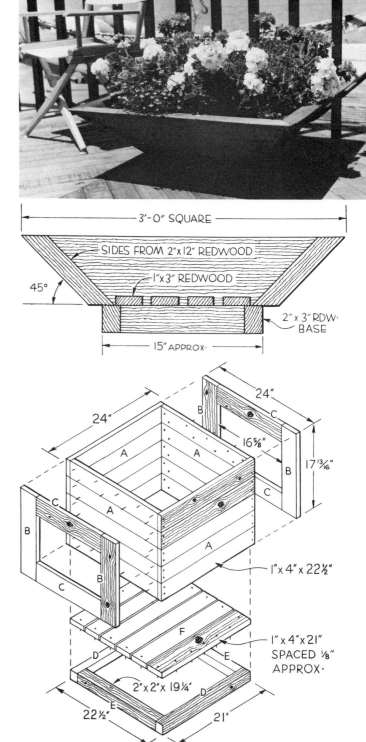

A garden without a garden: primroses, pansies, and emerging bulbs grow in handsome redwood planter boxes.

4
Flowering Plants

Regardless of where you live, most flowering plants for container gardening indoors and out can be classed as *tender perennial* or *annual*. "Tender perennial" means that the plant cannot survive freezing temperatures. The geranium of window gardens and boxes (actually a form of *Pelargonium*) makes a perfect example. Like many tender perennials, it can be grown from seed to bloom in a single growing season. In any climate where freezing occurs, the geranium—or any other tender perennial—will die unless brought indoors before frost in autumn. Plants in this category can be maintained all year in a coldframe, or indoors in a suitable environment, or they can be wintered indoors and summered out of doors. Where freezing temperatures never occur, these plants can be cultivated all year in the garden. In such a climate many tender perennials, geraniums included, may become large shrubs or even trees unless they are pruned back regularly.

An annual is a plant that grows from seed to bloom and produces seed with which to perpetuate itself all within a single growing season, then it dies. The zinnia is a good example.

Flowers

Group 1. Interestingly enough, the plants in the list below are members of the same family. They are gesneriads. All have fuzzy or hairy foliage that tends to become unsightly when subjected to

Group 1

Tender Perennial Flowers for Indoor Containers All Year or Outdoors in Warm Weather with Protection from Rain

LATIN NAME	POPULAR NAME
Part sun to shade	
Episcia	flame violet
Saintpaulia	African violet
Sinningia	gloxinia
Smithiantha	temple bells

Episcia dianthiflora *has fringed white flowers.*

wind and rain outdoors. They do make fine porch plants, however, during warm weather. The easiest way to get started with all of them is to buy established plants. These are available from many local florists and greenhouses, or you can send away to some of the specialists listed in Appendix A.

These gesneriads all need a warm, moist atmosphere and part sun to bright open shade. They grow to perfection in fluorescent-light gardens.

Hybrid sinningia (gloxinia) tubers available in the winter may be started into growth inside, then placed outdoors in a protected area when the weather is thoroughly warm. They will then flower all summer.

ABOVE: Tuberous begonia.
BELOW: Assorted achimenes.

Hybrid gloxinia four months after planting tuber.

Group 2. Among these tender perennials are some of the best of all flowering plants for container gardens, both indoors and out. According to their uses and growth habits, they can be further categorized as follows:

Tender bulbs. Those needing a good half day of sun include agapanthus, anemone, canna, crinum, dahlia, galtonia, hippeastrum, hymenocallis, lycoris, mont-

bretia, nerine, oxalis, ranunculus, spre-
kelia, tigridia, zephyranthes; for a place
with some shade, especially at midday,
achimenes, tuberous begonia, clivia, cyclamen, eucharis, eucomis, gloriosa, hae-
manthus, vallota and zantedeschia. Of
these, agapanthus and clivia are evergreen and can be kept growing year
round. All the others make leaf growth
and bloom, the foliage matures, and then
they require a period of dormancy during
which time the soil is kept nearly dry, no
fertilizer is applied, and the pots can be
stored in a dark but frost-free and mouse-
proof place. All may be planted in winter
or spring.

Hanging baskets. Almost any plant can
be put in a hanging container, but some
of the best cascaders and trailers require
some direct sun: *Abutilon megapotami-
cum variegatum*, antigonon, felicia, helio-
tropium, lantana, nierembergia, oxalis,
pelargonium (ivy-leaf types), petunia,
plumbago, verbena and vinca. For a place
protected from midday sun: achimenes,
aeschynanthus, tuberous begonia, browallia, columnea, fuchsia, hoya and impatiens.

Hot and dry. It is sometimes required
that outdoor container gardens be tolerant of hot, dry weather. Some of the
best ones from this list are: agapanthus,
Begonia semperflorens, canna, gazania,
lantana, pelargonium, tigridia and verbena. I do not mean to imply you can be
careless about watering these—only that
they won't die from being dry for a day
or two.

Availability. Although the Latin names
may not be familiar to you, if you will
read down the list of popular names I
am sure you will find many old acquaint-
ances. Most of these plants are commonly
available at local garden centers and
greenhouses. Some better and less common kinds and varieties may be found in
the catalogs of mail-order suppliers (see
listing of these firms in Appendix A).

*ABOVE: Hybrid amaryllis. BELOW: Impatiens 'Huck-
abuc.'*

Calla-lily semperflorens begonia has some white leaves.

Group 2

Tender Perennial Flowers for Outdoor Containers in Warm Weather, Indoors During Winter

Latin Name	Popular Name
Full sun	
Abutilon	flowering maple
Agapanthus	Lily of the Nile
Alstroemeria	Lily of Peru
Anemone	windflower
Antigonon	coral vine
Begonia	
semperflorens . . .	wax begonia
Canna	canna
Capsicum	ornamental pepper
Clianthus	glory pea
Clitoria	butterfly pea
Crinum	milk-and-wine lily
Cytisus	butcher's broom
Dahlia	dahlia
Datura	angel's trumpet
Dianthus	carnation; pink
Felicia	blue marguerite
Galtonia	Cape hyacinth
Gazania	gazania
Haemanthus	blood-lily
Heliotropium	heliotrope
Hibiscus	hibiscus
Hippeastrum	amaryllis
Hymenocallis	ismene; Peruvian daffodil
Jacobinia	king's crown
Lantana	lantana
Lycoris	spider lily
Montbretia	montbretia
Nerine	nerine
Nicotiana	flowering tobacco
Nierembergia	purple cups
Oxalis	oxalis
Oxypetalum	southern star
Pelargonium	geranium
Pentas	Egyptian star cluster
Petunia	petunia
Plumbago	plumbago
Phygelius	Cape fuchsia
Ranunculus	buttercup
Solanum	Christmas cherry
Sprekelia	sprekelia
Strelitzia	bird of paradise
Tigridia	tiger flower
Vallota	Scarborough lily
Verbena	verbena
Vinca	periwinkle
Zephyranthes	rain lily

Part sun to shade	
Achimenes	magic flower
Aeschynanthus	lipstick vine
Anthurium	Valentine flower
Aphelandra	zebra plant
Begonia	
semperflorens . . .	wax begonia
Begonia tuberosa . .	tuberous begonia
Bletilla	Chinese orchid
Browallia	Browallia
Clivia	Kafir lily
Columnea	columnea
Crossandra	crossandra
Cyclamen	shooting star
Eucharis	Amazon lily
Eucomis	pineapple lily
Fuchsia	fuchsia
Gesneria	gesneria
Gloriosa	climbing lily
Hoya	wax plant
Impatiens	patience plant
Orchidaceae	orchids
Streptocarpus	Cape primrose
Zantedeschia	calla-lily

Eucharis has fragrant white flowers.

Lemondrop marigold is easy to grow in containers.

Group 3. These are the annual flowers which are best suited to growing outdoors during warm weather. If you have a home greenhouse, you can also enjoy many of these for flowers in cold weather.

Hanging baskets. Excellent trailers and cascaders in this group (all facing good sunlight) include: calandrinia, cobaea, dimorphotheca, eccremocarpus, gypsophila, iberis, ipomoea, lathyrus, linaria, lobelia, lobularia, nemophila, *Phlox drummondi,* portulaca, reseda, schizanthus, tagetes, thunbergia, thymophylla, tropaeolum. Torenia will take a little shade.

Hot and dry. This group is rich in plants that can tolerate summer heat in outdoor containers. For example: agathaea, amaranthus, arctotis, bartonia, brachycome, calandrinia, calliopsis, centratherum, cladanthus, cleome, cosmos, dimorphotheca, emilia, eutoca, gaillardia, gomphrena, helianthus, lobularia, mirabilis, molucella, *Phlox drummondi,* portulaca, tagetes, tropaeolum, venidium, zanthisma and zinnia.

Availability. Common varieties are available as started plants at local nur-

series and garden centers at planting-out time in the spring. All of these, plus the rare and unusual can also be started early indoors from seeds, preferably 6 to 12 weeks ahead of warm weather.

Group 3

Annual Flowers for Outdoor Containers in Warm Weather

LATIN NAME	POPULAR NAME
Full sun	
Agathaea	blue daisy
Ageratum	floss flower
Amaranthus	Joseph's coat
Anchusa	summer forget-me-not
Antirrhinum	snapdragon
Arctotis	African daisy
Bartonia	blazing star
Brachycome	Swan River daisy
Brassica	flowering cabbage
Brassica	flowering kale
Calandrinia	succulent
Calendula	pot-marigold
Calliopsis	calliopsis
Callistephus	China aster
Celosia	cockscomb
Centaurea	bachelor's-button
Centratherum	Manaos beauty
Cerinthe	honeywort
Cladanthus	Palm Springs daisy
Clarkia	Rocky Mountain garland
Cleome	spider flower
Cobaea	cathedral bells
Cosmos	cosmos
Crepis	crepis
Crotalaria	crotalaria
Cuphea	firecracker plant
Delphinium	larkspur
Dimorphotheca	African daisy
Eccremocarpus	glory flower
Echium	viper's bugloss
Emilia	paintbrush
Eutoca	eutoca
Gaillardia	blanket flower

Godetia . . . . farewell to spring
Gomphrena . . . . everlasting
Gypsophila . . . . baby's-breath
Helianthus. . . . . . . sunflower
Helichrysum . . . . . strawflower
Iberis. . . . . annual candytuft
Ipomoea. . . . . morning glory
Impatiens
   balsamina . . . . . . balsam
Lathyrus . . . . sweet pea
Linaria . . . . linaria
Lobelia . . . . lobelia
Lobularia. . . . . sweet-alyssum
Machaerantha . . . . Tahoka daisy
Mathiola . . . . stock
Matricaria . . . . feverfew
Mimulus. . . . . monkey flower
Mirabilis . . . . four o'clock
Molucella. . . . . bells of Ireland
Nemesia. . . . . nemesia
Nemophila. . . . . . . baby blue eyes
Nigella. . . . . love-in-a-mist
Phlox drummondi . . annual phlox
Portulaca. . . . . rose moss
Reseda. . . . . mignonette
Salpiglossis. . . . . . . velvet flower
Scabiosa . . . . sweet scabious
Schizanthus. . . . . . butterfly flower
Statice. . . . . sea lavender
Tagetes . . . . marigold
Thunbergia . . . . . . black-eyed Susan
                      vine
Thymophylla. . . . . Dahlborg daisy
Tropaeolum. . . . . . nasturtium
Venidium. . . . . monarch of the
                      veldt
Verbesina . . . . butter daisy
Zanthisma. . . . . . . star of Texas
Zinnia . . . . zinnia

Part sun to shade
Cynoglossum. . . . . . Chinese forget-me-
                      not
Didiscus. . . . . lace flower
Myosotis . . . . forget-me-not
Nicotiana. . . . . flowering tobacco
Salvia . . . . flowering sage
Torenia . . . . wishbone flower

Group 4. These are the hardy perennial flowers, many of which form the very backbone of a perennial border. The ones suggested are excellent for container gardens. This grouping has been included with the city terrace and rooftop gardener especially in mind. Just because you live in the city, you don't have to limit your container gardening to geraniums and impatiens. It is true that the hardy perennials tend to be seasonal bloomers, but most offer attractive foilage both before and after flowering.

Group 4

Hardy Perennial Flowers for Outdoor Containers

(In cold climates, winter over by storing containers in a coldframe; or remove from containers and plant in the garden before winter freeze-up.)

LATIN NAME	POPULAR NAME
For sun	
Achillea.	yarrow
Alyssum	basket of gold
Arabis	rock cress
Armeria.	thrift; sea pink
Aubrieta	rock cress
Belamcanda.	blackberry lily
Bellis	English daisy
Catananche	cupid's dart
Cheiranthus.	wallflower
Chrysanthemum	mum and
	Shasta daisy
Coreopsis.	pot of gold
Delphinium	delphinium
Dianthus	carnation; pink
Doronicum.	leopard's bane
Erigeron	midsummer
	aster
Erinus	Alpine balsam
Eryngium	sea holly
Eupatorium	hardy
	ageratum
Gaillardia	blanket flower
Geum	geum

Hybrid, single-flowered chrysanthemum grown from seed makes a spectacular show during the same season.

Gypsophila . . . . baby's-breath
Helianthemum . . . . sun rose
Hemerocallis . . . . daylily
Heuchera . . . . coral bells
Hypericum . . . . St. John's-wort
Iberis . . . . perennial candytuft
Incarvillea . . . . hardy gloxinia
Iris . . . . iris
Lilium . . . . lily
Lunaria . . . . money plant
Monarda . . . . beebalm
Penstemon . . . . beard tongue
Phlox . . . . phlox
Physostegia . . . . obedient plant
Physalis . . . . Chinese lantern plant
Polemonium . . . . Jacob's ladder
Potentilla . . . . cinquefoil
Pyrethrum . . . . painted daisy
Rudbeckia . . . . gloriosa daisy
Scabiosa . . . . scabiosa

Stokesia . . . . Stokes' aster
Thalictrum . . . . meadowrue
Tritoma . . . . red hot poker
Trollius . . . . globeflower
Valeriana . . . . garden heliotrope
Veronica . . . . speedwell

Part sun to shade
Aquilegia . . . . columbine
Astilbe . . . . spirea
Bergenia . . . . saxifraga
Convallaria . . . . lily of the valley
Dicentra . . . . bleeding heart
Hosta . . . . plantain-lily
Liriope . . . . liriope
Mertensia . . . . Virginia bluebell
Primula . . . . primrose
Viola . . . . pansy; viola

Rex begonia leaves are like quilted brocade. This one combines silver, green, and burgundy coloring.

5
Foliage Plants

Plants included in this chapter are cultivated primarily for attractive foliage and often used in terrarium and bottle-garden plantings and as tabletop and window-sill decorations. Most can be kept indefinitely as small bushes or hanging-basket plants. The woody shrub-types are discussed in Chapter 6; foliage plants of tree size are in Chapter 7.

Foliage without Direct Sun

If you have a place that receives bright light, but no direct sun, here are some of the best plants from which to choose; these are the toughies that survive, even thrive, in the average house or office environment:

LATIN NAME	POPULAR NAME
Aglaonema	Chinese evergreen
Aspidistra	cast-iron plant
Beaucarnea	pony-tail
Brassaia	schefflera
Bromeliad	bromeliad
Ceropegia	hearts entangled
Chlorophytum	spider plant
Cissus	grape-ivy; kangaroo vine
Dieffenbachia	dumbcane
Dizygotheca	false aralia
Dracaena	corn plant
Fatsia	aralia
Filicineae	ferns
Hedera	English ivy
Hemigraphis	Red or flame ivy
Hoya	wax plant
Maranta	prayer plant
Pandanus	screw-pine

Pellionia	pellionia	*Cyperus*	umbrella plant
Peperomia	peperomia	*Euonymus*	euonymus
Philodendron	philodendron	*Ficus*	creeping fig
Pilea	artillery fern	*Fittonia*	fittonia
Pilea	aluminum plant	*Gynura*	purple passion
Plectranthus	Swedish-ivy	*Hoffmannia*	corduroy plant
Polyscias	aralia	*Homalomena*	homalomena
Rhoeo.	Moses in the cradle	*Hypoestes*	pink polka dot
Sansevieria	snake plant	*Ligularia*	leopard plant
Scindapsus	pothos	*Ophiopogon*	lily-turf
Spathiphyllum.	peace-lily	*Rhektophyllum*	rhektophyllum
Syngonium.	nephthytis	*Saxifraga.*	strawberry-begonia

In moderate to high humidity of 40 to 60 percent, you might grow any of the plants in the preceding list, plus these, many of which have beautiful multicolored foliage:

Scilla violacea.	scilla
Selaginella.	sweat plant
Sonerila	sonerila
Tolmiea	piggyback
Xanthosoma	xanthosoma
Zingiber.	ginger

LATIN NAME	POPULAR NAME
Acorus	miniature sweet flag
Alocasia	alocasia
Anthurium.	anthurium
Asparagus.	asparagus-fern
Begonia rex	rex begonia
Bertolonia	bertolonia
Calathea	calathea
Caladium.	caladium
Chamaeranthemum.	chamaeranthemum
Cordyline.	Hawaiian Ti
Ctenanthe	ctenanthe

Ctenanthe has leaves of many colors.

Best Foliage for Terrariums

From the two preceding lists, my favorite foliage plants for terrariums and bottle gardens are the ones that stay fairly small naturally. These include: cryptanthus (a bromeliad), miniature spider plant (*Chlorophytum bichetti*), many ferns, small-leaved English ivies, pellionia, peperomia, *Philodendron sodiroi*, acorus, *Anthurium clarinervum,* miniature varieties of rex begonia, berto*lonia,* small varieties of calathea, chamaeranthemum, euonymus, creeping fig, fittonia, saxifraga, *Scilla violacea*, selaginella and sonerila.

For a terrarium or bottle garden that receives bright reflected light most of the day—but little or no direct sun—or one cultivated in a fluorescent-light garden, you might add to my list of foliage plants these little plants that also flower: *Allophyton mexicanum* (Mexican foxglove), *Begonia prismatocarpa,* 'Cygnet' episcia, *Gesneria cuneifolia* and its hybrids, miniature African violets, *Seemannia latifolia* and *Sinningia pusilla* and other miniature gloxinias.

ABOVE: Cryptanthus, miniature relative of the pine-apple.

BELOW, LEFT: Maranta foliage. RIGHT: Anthurium clarinervum.

BELOW: Miniature rex begonias have such colorful leaves, they can take the place of flowers in terrariums.

Fancyleaf geraniums have colorful leaves, as well as flowers.

ABOVE: Silvery dusty miller foliage.
BELOW: Hostas make striking plants in containers outdoors.

BELOW: Coleus grows in the colors of a Persian carpet.

Colorful Foliage for Outdoors

In this grouping you will find plants with beautifully colored leaves, and these tend to do best as outdoor container plants. Indoors, lack of sufficient sun is often a problem, especially during the winter months. Of these, most notable are coleus, perilla, fancyleaf geraniums and any of the silvery-leaved dusty millers (*Senecio cineraria,* for example). Hosta makes a handsome foliage plant in containers outdoors in the summer but requires wintering over in a cold place (planted back in the garden, or in a coldframe). Fancy-leaved caladiums grow from bulbs; plant these in a warm, moist place indoors in the spring, then transfer outdoors when the weather settles and there is no possible danger of frost.

Succulent sedums and sempervivums make great-looking container plants outdoors in a sunny place. In mild climates they can be left outdoors unprotected all year. Where temperatures go below 20 degrees F. they should be wintered over in a cool room or coldframe.

Favorite coleus plants can easily be kept from one outdoor season to another, either by cutting back the old stems or by rooting tip cuttings and carrying these over winter indoors in a sunny window or in a fluorescent-light garden. Coleus, dusty miller and perilla may be started indoors from seeds six to ten weeks before planting-out time in the spring.

6
Shrubs

Virtually all shrubs and vines with more or less woody stems can be cultivated in container gardens. If the plant grows outdoors in the ground year round in your climate, then you can also try it in a good-sized tub or wooden planter box. Where freezing temperatures occur, it is vital that soil in the container go into winter freeze-up in a moist condition. It follows that pottery containers should not be left out in the winter, because frozen soil expands and the result will be cracked pottery. Often concrete containers do not break, owing to their strength and bowl-shaped bottoms.

If you have an outdoor garden in the North, I am going to assume you have all the common shrubs like lilacs and forsythia you want growing in the ground, and that your interest in container shrubs will be for more exotic tropicals. However, if you have only a terrace or rooftop garden in the North, there is no reason not to try your most favorite woody shrubs, evergreens and vines as part of a container garden.

Cold-sensitive (Below 45°) Shrubs for Containers

The plants in this category are mostly common and everyday in the tropics, but the only way to really enjoy them in up-North gardens is to take advantage of container plantings. In warm weather they can be wheeled outdoors, but when frost threatens they need a warm place inside. This doesn't have to be a greenhouse or sun porch, although either place makes a fine winter home for these plants. You can keep them in any cold-free space—perhaps a garage or basement, or simply within the light range of a bright window. Hot, dry heat in the winter is not to the liking of any of them.

Availability. In the South you will find most of these at your local nursery or garden center. In the North you may or may not. The widespread popularity of container gardening has encouraged Northern nurserymen to stock more and more tropical shrubs.

Young plants of most of these are also available through mail-order specialists whose names and addresses are listed in Appendix A.

LATIN NAME	POPULAR NAME
Allamanda	golden trumpet
Ardisia	coral berry
Bambusa	bamboo
Begonia, cane or angel-wing	begonia
Bougainvillea	paper flower
Calliandra	powderpuff
Callistemon	bottlebrush
Camellia	camellia
Carissa	natal-plum
Clerodendrum	Bleeding-heart vine
Clerodendrum	Cashmere bouquet
Codiaeum	croton
Daphne	daphne
Dipladenia	dipladenia
Eugenia	Surinam cherry
Fatshedera	fatshedera
Gardenia	gardenia
Hibiscus	hibiscus
Ixora	ixora
Jasminum	jasmine
Ligustrum	ligustrum
Mahonia	mahonia
Malpighia	Barbados cherry
Nerium	oleander
Osmanthus	sweet-olive
Passiflora	passion flower
Pittosporum	pittosporum
Podocarpus	podocarpus
Stephanotis	stephanotis vine
Tecomaria	Cape honey-suckle

ABOVE: Golden allamanda. BELOW: Pots of fragrant jasmine.

ABOVE: Vivid bougainvillea. BELOW: Sweet Daphne odora.

'Mrs. Roeding' oleander flowers readily in containers.

How to Grow Potted Camellias

The year-round schedule for growing camellias in pots or tubs is partly like that for other cold-sensitive shrubs. There are some distinct differences, however, and since camellias are among the most beautiful of shrubs to grow in containers, specific instructions are included here. The suggestions that follow, prepared by the U.S. Department of Agriculture, tell how best to succeed with camellias, but also give ideas for how to handle other tender shrubs in containers.

Camellias can be grown in containers indefinitely if they are given the proper care. Their requirements are essentially the same as for plants grown outdoors—partial shade, adequate moisture, rich soil and good drainage.

If the plant you buy from the nursery is container-grown, you need not transplant it unless you want a more attractive container. Nursery plants are usually potted in good soil. If your plant out-grows its container, you can transplant it at any time of the year.

Use a potting soil made of one-fourth woods leaf mold, one-fourth sand and one-half peat moss. Place a one-inch layer of gravel at the bottom of the new container to provide drainage.

Water the plants heavily, then allow the soil to dry moderately before watering again. The critical period in watering occurs in spring, when the plants are growing rapidly. They need much more water then than at any other time of the year.

During the hot summer months, spray the leaves with water every afternoon. Spraying keeps the air humid around the plants.

Fertilize potted plants monthly throughout the year. For monthly feedings from March through July, use a liquid fertilizer, analysis 15-5-5. In August through February use a 7-6-19 liquid fertilizer. Do not overfertilize; it is better to feed too little than too much. Never fertilize a dry plant.

Potted camellias may be pruned any time of the year to control their size and maintain their shape. When cutting a bloom, take two or three leaves with it. This will help to maintain the shape of the plant.

You may want to disbud your plant to obtain large specimen blooms. The best time to disbud is when you are able to distinguish the flower bud from the growth bud. For early blooming varieties, disbudding is best done in September or October.

To disbud, use a large pin or a shingle nail to pierce a hole from the tip of the bud downward. This allows air to enter the bud so it will dry and fall off naturally, thus eliminating possible injury to the adjoining bud that you want to keep.

In some parts of southern California, southern Texas and Florida, potted camellias can be left outdoors all winter. In other areas it is best to move them

ABOVE: Crape-myrtlette flowers profusely in pots.

ABOVE: Azaleas grow well in pots. BELOW: Clematis.

in winter to some place where their roots will be protected from freezing.

They can be taken indoors and will bloom there if the room temperatures can be kept between 35 and 50 degrees F. and the humidity held reasonably high.

Hardy Shrubs for Containers

In this category, please take the designation "hardy" with a grain of salt. If the shrub grows well in your community without special winter protection, then you will probably have no difficulty growing it outdoors all year in a container, providing the soil about the roots goes into winter freeze-up in a well-moistened condition. If the shrub is of doubtful winter hardiness in your climate when planted in a desirable spot in the ground, then you cannot hope to bring it through winter as a container plant in the open. Move it to an interior space where it will have some protection—for example, a garage, basement or cool room where there is light.

Availability. Most if not all of these shrubs may be found already growing in containers in local nurseries and garden centers. For unusual varieties you may find it best to send away to a specialist; see names and addresses in Appendix A.

LATIN NAME	POPULAR NAME
Aucuba	golddust plant
Campsis	trumpet vine/bush
Clematis	clematis vine
Cotoneaster	rockspray
Ilex	holly
Juniperus	juniper
Lagerstroemia	crape-myrtle
Nandina	heavenly bamboo
Pyracantha	firethorn
Rhododendron	rhododendron
Rhododendron	azalea
Rosa	rose
Viburnum	viburnum
Wisteria	wisteria

Trees ⁷

One of the nicest influences of container gardening has been the widespread planting of trees in large tubs and planters. At first we saw them greening and shading open public spaces, but gradually they have moved inside. A few years ago it was unusual to see a tree indoors, spreading its branches out and upward to the ceiling. Now no living space seems quite finished without a tree-size plant. The idea has been nurtured along by environmentalists, architects, decorators and by young people seeking to get closer to nature. It is now universally accepted as the right and good thing to do, indoors and outdoors.

Trees to plant in containers outdoors need not be expensive at all, especially if you begin in the spring with a dormant, bare-root specimen from a mail-order nursery. However, the best trees for growing year round as houseplants tend to be relatively expensive. The one exception is an avocado, which you can grow to tree size in two years for practically no investment at all. After all, you bought the avocado to eat; the seed pit is a true bonus. For how to start an avocado, see Chapter 1.

The Best Indoor Trees

All of the tree-size plants cultivated in containers as houseplants are incapable of withstanding freezing temperatures or even cold exposed sites. You can move them outdoors in warm weather, but they should be brought back inside well ahead of frost in autumn.

Araucaria excelsa. Norfolk Island pine. This cold-tender needle evergreen is available in all sizes from a two-and-a-half-inch pot seedling to a real ceiling pusher (the latter for quite a high price, incidentally). It needs bright light, preferably with a little direct sun. Keep the soil evenly moist. It can't stand being hot and dry at the same time.

Norfolk Island pine makes a graceful indoor tree.

Brassaia actinophylla. Schefflera. Available in all sizes from seedlings and rooted cuttings to towering trees. Little schefflera plants grow rapidly in the right conditions; no matter how small one appears, it is a mistake to plant it in a terrarium or dish garden. Schefflera grows well in bright light, although a little direct sun won't hurt indoors. Water the soil really well, then not again until the surface feels almost dry to your fingers.

Chamaedorea erumpens. Bamboo palm. A graceful palm with strong vertical lines; it may well remind you more of a clump of bamboo than a palm. It tolerates low light, but does best in light you might read or do needlework by. Keep the soil evenly moist. The related, and more common dwarf or Neanthe bella palm, *Chamaedorea elegans,* seldom grows taller than four feet indoors, but one of this size placed on top of a stool or pedestal can give the effect of a tree indoors.

Chamaerops humilis. European fan palm. This tree is wider-spreading than the bamboo palm. In fact, the specimens most often available in Northern shops seem to be widest in girth right at eye level. You can solve this problem by elevating the pot on a footstool, low table or some other kind of pedestal so that the branches spread high enough for you to walk under them. This palm needs as much light as possible. Keep the soil evenly moist.

Dieffenbachia amoena. Dumbcane. This big tropical plant is not really a tree with spreading branches, but in terms of leaf volume, you can buy a lot of green for relatively little money when you invest in a large dieffenbachia. Give it medium light, preferably a little direct sun indoors. Water well, then not again until the surface soil feels almost dry.

LEFT: *Brassaia (schefflera) grows to ceiling height.*
ABOVE: *Dwarf palm grows to four feet tall indoors.*
BELOW: *Pale green dieffenbachia and large philo-*
  dendron.

Loquat tree in tub will survive winters indoors if it receives some sun outdoors in warm weather

Dizygotheca elegantissima. Spider aralia. This is the plant with leaves that look like marijuana; in fact, people have been known to ask shopkeepers for "the one that looks like marijuana." It thrives in as much light as you can give it, but direct sun is not required. The dizygotheca, like most related plants in the aralia family, resents being moved. It will lose some leaves, but if you care for it properly and leave it in one place, it will adapt. Keep the soil evenly moist at all times.

Dracaena fragrans. Corn plant. Like the dieffenbachia, this dracaena tends to be more of a big bush than a tree. However, it does give a mass of fresh green foliage, and this plant is one of the most tolerant of all of low light and neglect. For best results, keep the soil in a range from evenly moist to wet; however, it won't keel over and die if you forget to water it for a few days.

Dracaena marginata. Dragon tree. This plant is characterized by tall, slender trunks or branches that often curve and zigzag in an interesting if not bizarre fashion. These are topped by tufts or plumes of narrow green leaves banded in dark red. Give it medium light; direct sun is not needed. Keep the soil in a range from evenly moist to wet. Each time you forget to water and the soil dries out severely, many of the older leaves will turn yellow and fall off.

Eriobotrya japonica. Japanese loquat. This plant has rather coarse leaves, but it makes an excellent indoor tree. In the Northeast, at least, I have never seen it offered in a plant shop, but it is widely cultivated in the Los Angeles area. It needs some direct sun indoors. Keep the soil evenly moist.

Ficus benjamina exotica. Weeping Java fig. Probably the most popular of all indoor trees, especially among designers and decorators. It is always graceful and

ABOVE: Characteristically bizarre Dracaena marginata.
BELOW: Ficus benjamina exotica, *the weeping fig tree.*

Ficus elastica decora, *an improved rubber tree.*

Ficus lyrata, *fiddleleaf fig, is an excellent tree.*

tends to develop wide-spreading branches which you can sit under indoors and easily make believe you are resting under a marvelous old shade tree outdoors. It needs strong light indoors, but direct sun is not necessary. Keep the soil evenly moist.

Ficus elastica decora. Rubber plant. This fig has much bolder leaves than *F. benjamina,* and it is never as graceful, especially in a relatively small space. However, it is not terribly expensive nor is it temperamental. Give it medium light but little or no direct sun (which tends to burn holes in the leaves). Keep the soil evenly moist.

Ficus lyrata. Fiddleleaf fig. This fig is even bolder in appearance than the rubber plant, but it often succeeds in being more graceful. Culture is the same.

Other tree-size figs to grow indoors include *Ficus philippinensis* (Philippine fig), *F. retusa nitida* (Indian laurel), which lends itself well to training and clipping into a formal tree, and *F. triangularis,* which has triangle-shape leaves and has only recently begun to appear in commerce.

Howeia forsteriana. Kentia palm. If you want a big Victorian-looking palm, this is the one to search out. It is in great demand and is apparently somewhat difficult to propagate. Therefore, expect to pay more than you would for the ubiquitous and temperamental areca palm.

Ficus triangularis *has triangular leaves.*

A young kentia, perhaps the best large indoor palm.

However, the kentia is worth every penny. It grows beautifully and easily indoors if you give it half a chance. Provide low to medium light; little or no direct sun is needed. Keep the soil evenly moist.

Ligustrum lucidum. Waxleaf privet. Like *Ficus retusa nitida,* this is amenable to training and trimming into a neat, rather formal appearance. Give it medium light. Water well, then not again until the surface soil begins to feel dry. However, don't expect this privet to thrive indoors in winter in hot, dry heat.

Podocarpus macrophylla maki. Podocarpus. This is a handsome evergreen tree for indoors, with older leaves a dark

green, the newer ones pale chartreuse. It will tolerate light indoors from sunny to shady. Keep the soil evenly moist. In the winter, try not to situate it where hot, dry heat blows on the branches.

Rhapis excelsa. Lady palm. This graceful palm makes a beautiful indoor tree. Give it medium light; little or no direct sun is needed. Keep the soil in a range from evenly moist to wet.

Fitting Trees to Containers

Any of the indoor trees suggested here will grow in a 12- to 14-inch pot or tub until it is about six feet tall, then it will need an 18-inch container for best growth. If an indoor tree really does become a

Japanese maple grown to perfection in a container.

ceiling pusher, prune out the top and repot in the same container in which it has been growing; simply remove part of the old soil, clip away some of the old roots, and add fresh soil.

One problem you may experience with large indoor trees is keeping the foliage clean. If you can put one in the bathtub and give it a shower of tepid water, you have no problem. Or if you can put it outdoors for a shower from the hose in warm weather, the leaves can be cleaned with relative ease. Otherwise, you can take a damp cloth and clean individual leaves if they are large enough to make this feasible, or you can use a feather duster for small leaves like those of *Ficus benjamina exotica.*

Trees for Outdoor Containers

Any of the tropical trees suggested for growing indoors can also be grown outdoors—all year in frost-free climates, during warm weather in the North.

Since all local nurseries carry a stock of young trees in containers, it will pay you to look around and see what is available in your own community. If you live in a cold climate and want to leave a container tree outdoors all year, containerize only those known to be the hardiest.

Keeping the soil moist at all times is the greatest problem with containerized trees outdoors. Rainfall is seldom sufficient in any climate. You really have to be the rainmaker. If you have a container tree that always seems to be dry, it probably needs more soil in which to spread its roots. Outdoor trees tend to need larger containers than those indoors. A flowering crab apple approximately six feet tall with a branch spread of perhaps six feet will need a container two to three feet in diameter and 18 to 24 inches deep minimum. Indoors a tree of this size would do nicely in an 18-inch pot.

8
Vegetables, Herbs and Fruit

Herbs have been grown in containers for hundreds of years, but only recently have we realized that not only can vegetables be beautiful but they too can be grown in pots, tubs, plastic-lined fruit baskets, garbage pails and even in hanging baskets. Among fruit, strawberries, dwarf citrus and dwarf peaches of the Bonanza variety in particular are especially suited to container gardening.

To grow herbs indoors you will need a window that receives full sun for at least half of the day. With this same amount of sun, but in cooler temperatures—preferably not over 60 degrees F.—you can also grow a fairly decent crop of leaf lettuce. If you have no sun, then a fluorescent-light garden will give you a place to grow herbs and a few salad greens. Dwarf citrus can be a fine houseplant, but strawberries and dwarf peaches are best left to the outdoor garden.

Herbs Indoors and Outdoors

Some herbs are grown primarily for seasoning, others for good scents. Among the favorites for culinary purposes are sweet basil, chives, dill, oregano, parsley, rosemary, thyme, sage, various mints, savory, sweet bay and tarragon. Others you may want to try include anise, borage, caraway, chervil, Florence fennel and sweet marjoram.

Herbs cultivated primarily—or entirely—for the good scents they give off, especially when a leaf is squeezed, include lavender, catnip (used, of course, for making tea), and scented geraniums. Besides the fairly common rose-scented geranium there are varieties with the fragrance of nutmeg, apple, lemon, coconut, pineapple, orange and pungent.

Young plants of all these herbs may be found at some local nurseries and garden centers in the spring. Occasionally they may also be found in autumn. Mail-order herb specialists (listed in Appendix A) will ship plants almost any season the weather permits. You can also grow many fine herbs from seeds. Some of the easier ones to start this way include basil, chives, dill, parsley, anise, borage, caraway, marjoram, fennel and summer savory.

If you're a good container gardener who never forgets to water, you should be able to keep sweet bay, rosemary and lemon-verbena indefinitely. As container plants, they should not be left out of doors in freezing weather, however. The best place for them in the winter is a cool, sunny place where temperatures seldom go above 68 degrees F. Hot, dry artificial heat is not to their liking.

Whether you are growing herbs in natural or fluorescent light, keep snipping them back, both for seasoning and to promote more compact growth.

Herbs used alone, or in combination with pots and other planters of flowers, make handsome container gardens outdoors in warm weather. Foliage colors vary from silvery gray to dark green to burgundy, in texture from filmy and feathery to broad and bold.

Outdoors, herbs need at least a half day of sunlight for best growth. Water them really well, then not again until the surface soil begins to feel dry.

In cold climates, containers of the hardy perennial herbs (catnip, lavender, thyme, sweet woodruff, tarragon, winter savory, sage, mint and chives) can be wintered over with the pots sunk to the rims in sand or peat moss in a coldframe or other protected place. A sun-heated pit greenhouse, described in Chapter 1, provides a great environment for cultivating all kinds of herbs in the winter.

Young potted herbs ready for first clippings. Left to right: chives, sweet basil, rosemary, and oregano.

Vegetables in Containers, Indoors and Out

Vegetables are not exactly superstars among houseplants, but there are a few with which you may be successful in a sunny window or in a fluorescent-light garden.

Perhaps the best is Curlycress, which will grow from seed packet to salad and sandwich garnish in ten days. Make sowings at any season approximately every two weeks. The dark green, finely cut and curled leaves are similar to parsley. If you have a cool window, try watercress. It is a slower crop (allow about 50 days from planting) and should be cultivated in a large, shallow container of soil with the saucer kept filled with water at all times.

Lettuce would make a fine houseplant were it not for the fact that it loves cool weather. If you have a cool, sunny room, or can build a fluorescent-light garden in a cool room or basement, you may be successful with any of the leaf lettuces such as Ruby, Green Ice and Oak Leaf. If you are growing only lettuce and seasoning herbs in a fluorescent-light garden, you may wish to experiment with continuous lighting. Although this procedure will not work where flowering plants are involved (they need properly balanced periods of light and dark within every 24 hours), it is definitely worth trying where leaf growth is the only kind desired.

Small hot peppers and cherry tomatoes are also sometimes cultivated indoors in a sunny place or under fluorescent lights burned 16 hours out of every 24. They are naturally warm-weather plants, so the indoor environment is no great challenge for them.

In an indoor environment suited to lettuce, you might also try a few pots of radishes. Planted in pots of a spongy

ABOVE: Patio Pik hybrid cucumber in hanging basket.
BELOW: Patio hybrid tomato thriving in large pot.

ABOVE: *Fruit baskets and boxes lined with polyethylene plastic and filled with potting soil provide a ready and inexpensive place for growing vegetables. Kinds include lettuce, radishes, cabbage, scallions, and colorful rhubarb chard. Containers of marigolds and flowering sage complete the picture.*
LEFT: *Sweet pepper thrives as a container plant.*

soil-less medium (see Chapter 13) and fed lightly with each watering, they will do nicely.

If the container is large enough, you can grow any vegetable this way outdoors. All of them need at least a half day of sunlight and generous watering and feeding.

In terms of their decorative appearance and edible harvest, some of the most rewarding vegetables to grow in containers outdoors are rhubarb chard, Swiss chard, eggplant, dwarf or patio type cucumbers and tomatoes, leaf lettuce, okra (in climates with a long, warm season), peppers, Malabar spinach and zucchini.

The only real problem with vegetables in containers is letting the soil dry out between waterings. If the plants wilt, then you've waited too long to give them a drink and the harvest will be nonexistent or of poor quality. If you are growing any vegetable in an individual pot 12 inches in diameter or smaller, you may find it advantageous in really hot weather to place the pot inside a larger container and then fill the space between with moist peat moss. This will help keep roots cooler and also prevent the soil from drying out so rapidly.

The Potted Orchard

Strawberries as well as most dwarf and bush fruits can be cultivated in containers out of doors. Perhaps most outstanding are strawberries of the runnerless, *fraises des bois* type. One of these, Baron Solemacher, is easily cultivated from seeds started indoors in late winter, then transplanted outdoors in the spring. The seedlings will bear fruit that same summer. The dwarf Bonanza peach is the best choice for containers, and all kinds of dwarf citrus are well suited to this way of gardening. In severely cold climates both strawberries and Bonanza peach should be wintered over in a protected environment where temperatures will not fall below 20 degrees F. Dwarf citrus should not be subjected to frost, but this is no real problem in any climate since they adapt fairly well to any bright, preferably sunny, indoor environment.

If you have the space and the inclination, there is no reason not to try any number of other fruits in containers outdoors. These include everbearing fig (winter over in a place where temperatures do not fall below 20 degrees F.), dwarf apple, dwarf pear, dwarf plum, dwarf apricot, dwarf cherry and dwarf nectarine. Also blueberries, raspberries and hybrid table grapes.

Dwarf citrus flower and fruit are in these planter boxes.

Spider plant makes a graceful subject for hanging-basket culture indoors and outdoors.

9
Hanging Baskets, Window Boxes and Urns

The plants that naturally trail, creep, cascade or climb are ideal choices for hanging baskets, urns and other pedestal-displayed containers and outdoor window boxes. In recent years hanging baskets have all but replaced draperies and curtains in many houses and apartments.

Indoors, brackets for holding hanging baskets can be mounted on walls or frames near the window, or the baskets can be suspended from ceiling hooks. Indoors the major problems with hanging baskets are lack of light and winter heat—which naturally rises to the ceiling, where it tends to dry out basket plants, especially kinds that prefer temperatures on the cool side.

Outdoors, hanging baskets can be suspended from hooks installed in overhanging eaves, from tree branches and porch ceilings. Some arbors are built solely for them. Brackets can be mounted on walls, fences and posts. The main problem with hanging baskets, outdoors is too much exposure to hot, dry winds.

Of major concern for basket gardening indoors and outdoors is hanging them so they are absolutely secure. There is nothing quite so disappointing as to find that the wind has blown a perfectly beautiful hanging tuberous begonia from its perch and left it strewn about the terrace or porch. And indoors it is not a pleasant chore to clean up the mess left by a basket that has fallen from a poorly installed ceiling hook or other means of display.

Containers for Hanging Plants

The best hanging baskets for indoors are those with some means of catching excess moisture. Outdoors, where dripping water is of little concern, the time-honored wire baskets make excellent containers, as do redwood boxes and cradles. At your local garden center you will also find a variety of plastic hanging containers. The white hanging pots with an attached saucer have been sold by the millions in recent years. If your color scheme includes white, they may be fine. Otherwise, you may wish to cover them with inexpensive woven baskets.

To suspend hanging containers you can use nylon cord, wire or special macramé holders.

If you want an almost-instant effect from hanging-basket plants, you may prefer to buy established specimens. However, many of the ones sold by local florists have reached peak growth and will be difficult to keep in good condition. The best way is to grow your own basket plantings, starting from seeds, cuttings or young plants.

For planting a hanging container, use only a growing medium that is light and spongy and holds moisture well. You might use a mix composed of two parts sphagnum peat moss to one part each of garden loam and sand. Or you can use a mixture of equal parts garden loam, sphagnum peat moss and vermiculite. In recent years the soil-less mixes have become popular for hanging-basket plantings. These are marketed under such names as Vita-Bark University Mix, Jiffy Mix, Redi-Earth and Supersoil. If you grow in soil-less, however, be prepared to feed a little with almost every watering (see Chapter 13).

If you are using a porous basket, for example, a container constructed of wire or wooden slats, or an open-work plastic container, line it completely with unmilled sphagnum moss or florist's sheet moss before you add potting soil. After you finish planting such a container, immerse it in a pail, sink or tub of water for a good soaking; remove, allow to drain; then hang it in the growing place. If a hanging basket of this type is never allowed to dry out severely, you will not need to remove it for soaking. However, if such a basket dries out severely, remove it, soak in a container of water, allow to drain, and then hang it back up.

Hanging baskets indoors will need to be turned a quarter or half turn once each week in order for all growth to receive a uniform amount of light.

Whether indoors or outdoors, hanging-basket plants will grow best if you are attentive to pinching back tips. This encourages compact, full growth. Rapid-growing indoor basket plants such as Swedish-ivy and wandering Jew in particular need almost weekly pinching back in order to keep them dense and healthy.

One word of caution: plants suspended in the air tend to dry out much more rapidly than those resting on the floor, a window sill or a surface outdoors. Baskets that receive full sun outdoors in the summer may need to be watered well twice a day, once in the morning, once in the evening.

Best Houseplants for Hanging Baskets

In the lists that follow I have divided the best and most popular hanging-basket plants according to their light requirements. Some are so adaptable, I have listed them in more than one category. Also light is tremendously variable from climate to climate, according to the time of the year and many other factors. If any hanging-basket plant wilts daily or develops burned, yellowed leaves, you will know it needs less direct sun. If, on the other hand, a basket plant looks pale, drops a great many older leaves, and new growth is weak, more direct sun is probably needed.

Burro's-tail Sedum morganianum *as a hanging basket.*

Baskets for sun

LATIN NAME	POPULAR NAME
Abutilon megapotamicum	flowering-maple
Aeschynanthus	lipstick vine
Asparagus	asparagus-fern
Begonia	begonia
Bromeliad	bromeliad
Campanula isophylla	star of Bethlehem
Ceropegia	hearts entangled; rosary vine
Chlorophytum	spider plant
Cissus	grape-ivy
Coleus	coleus
Columnea	columnea
Epiphyllum	orchid cactus
Episcia	flame violet
Helxine	baby's-tears
Hoya	wax plant
Hypocyrta	goldfish plant
Ipomoea	sweet potato
Kalanchoe	kalanchoe
Mahernia	honeybells
Maranta	prayer plant
Orchidaceae	orchids
Oxalis	oxalis
Passiflora	passion flower
Pilea	pilea
Plectranthus	Swedish-ivy
Polypodiaceae	ferns
Rhipsalis	rhipsalis
Schizocentron	Spanish shawl
Schlumbergera	Christmas cactus
Sedum	donkey-tail
Streptosolen	orange browallia
Tradescantia	wandering Jew
Zygocactus	Thanksgiving cactus

Baskets for sun/shade

LATIN NAME	POPULAR NAME
Achimenes	magic flower
Aeschynanthus	lipstick vine
Bromeliad	bromeliad
Calathea	calathea
Ceropegia	hearts entangled; rosary vine

Pellionia makes a beautiful basket in a shady place.

Chlorophytum	spider plant
Cissus	grape-ivy
Columnea	columnea
Cymbalaria	Kenilworth-ivy
Episcia	flame violet
Ficus pumila	creeping fig
Hoya	wax plant
Hypocyrta	goldfish plant
Manettia	manettia
Maranta	prayer plant
Pellionia	pellionia
Peperomia	peperomia
Philodendron	philodendron
Pilea	pilea
Polypodiaceae	ferns
Schizocentron	Spanish shawl
Scindapsus	pothos
Selaginella	sweat plant
Senecio	German ivy
Syngonium	trileaf wonder
Tradescantia	wandering Jew

Indoor Baskets Outdoors

In warm weather, any of the house-plants suggested for hanging baskets may be enjoyed out of doors in a suitable place. Remember, when you take any houseplant outdoors, it needs a period of adjustment to the open environment, especially protection from midday sun and hot, dry winds.

Indoor baskets for outdoor sun

LATIN NAME	POPULAR NAME
Abutilon megapotamicum	flowering-maple
Asparagus	asparagus-fern
Bromeliad	bromeliad
Ceropegia	hearts entangled; rosary vine
Chlorophytum	spider plant
Ipomoea	morning glory
Kalanchoe	*Kalanchoe*
Oxalis	oxalis
Passiflora	passion flower
Sedum	donkey-tail
Streptosolen	orange browallia

Indoor baskets for outdoor shade

LATIN NAME	POPULAR NAME
Aeschynanthus	lipstick vine
Begonia	begonia
Bromeliad	bromeliad
Calathea	calathea
Campanula	star of Bethlehem
Ceropegia	hearts entangled; rosary vine
Chlorophytum	spider plant
Cissus	grape-ivy
Coleus	coleus
Columnea	columnea
Cymbalaria	Kenilworth ivy
Episcia	flame violet
Epiphyllum	orchid cactus
Ficus pumila	creeping fig
Helxine	baby's-tears
Hoya	wax plant
Hypocyrta	goldfish plant
Mahernia	honeybells
Manettia	manettia
Maranta	prayer plant
Orchidaceae	orchids
Oxalis	oxalis
Passiflora	passion flower
Pellionia	pellionia
Peperomia	peperomia
Philodendron	philodendron
Pilea	pilea
Plectranthus	Swedish-ivy
Polypodiaceae	ferns
Rhipsalis	rhipsalis
Schizocentron	Spanish shawl
Schlumbergera	Christmas cactus
Scindapsus	pothos
Sedum	donkey-tail
Selaginella	sweat plant
Senecio	German ivy
Streptosolen	orange browallia
Syngonium	trileaf wonder
Tradescantia	wandering Jew
Zygocactus	Thanksgiving cactus

Best Annuals for Outdoor Baskets

The plants in this category are either annuals or tender perennials. All of them can be started from seeds or cuttings in late winter or early spring indoors and then transplanted to hanging baskets, urns or window boxes when the weather is warm.

Fuchsias are breathtaking hanging-basket flowers.

Outdoor baskets for sun

LATIN NAME	POPULAR NAME
Ageratum	floss-flower
Antirrhinum, dwarf...	snapdragon
Begonia semperflorens	wax begonia
Beloperone.........	shrimp plant
Browallia..........	browallia
Coleus	coleus
Convolvulus........	morning glory
Dianthus	pinks
Dimorphotheca	African daisy
Fuchsia	fuchsia
Lantana...........	lantana
Lobelia	lobelia
Lobularia..........	sweet-alyssum
Mimulus.	monkey flower
Nemesia...........	nemesia
Nierembergia	cup-flower
Pelargonium	geranium
Petunia	petunia
Phacelia...........	phacelia
Phlox drummondi	annual phlox
Plumbago	plumbago
Portulaca..........	rose-moss
Tropaeolum........	nasturtium
Verbena...........	verbena

Outdoor baskets for sun/shade

LATIN NAME	POPULAR NAME
Begonia semperflorens	wax begonia
Begonia tuberhybrida	tuberous, cascade begonia
Browallia..........	browallia
Coleus	coleus
Fuchsia	fuchsia
Impatiens	sultana
Lobelia	lobelia
Mimulus.	monkey flower
Nemesia...........	nemesia
Nierembergia	cup-flower
Phacelia...........	phacelia
Torenia	wishbone-flower
Vinca.............	periwinkle

Cascade-type petunias are superstar basket plants.

If you want hanging baskets, boxes and urns outdoors filled with cascades of flowers early in the spring, plant them with candytuft, English daisies, forget-me-nots, pansies and other violas and wallflower. These will expire when really hot weather hits, and then you'll have to replace them. I also use English primroses in these containers in early spring and then transplant them to a shaded, moist part of the garden until basket-planting time the following year.

Any of the annual climbing vines can be used, one of a kind to each basket. You'll have to do some training to keep the vines from trying to climb too much; just keep winding them around and around the basket. Kinds include black-eyed-Susan vine, canary-bird vine, cardinal climber, cypress vine, morning glory and sweet pea. Herbs, also, can be grown in hanging baskets, window boxes. and urns, as can cherry tomatoes and the patio-type dwarf cucumbers.

If you grow them through the spring and summer in some out-of-the-way part of your garden, cascade-type chrysanthemums will be the glory of autumn as hanging baskets.

The dwarf pomegranate is one of the best of all bonsai subjects for cultivating all year indoors.

10
Bonsai and Other Art Forms

Container plants offer exciting possibilities beyond the rewards of flowers, foliage, fragrance and fruit. They can become living art forms that offer endless hours of pleasure. Some of these specialized techniques are described in illustrations here.

Miniature Trees the Bonsai Way

In recent years the ancient Oriental art of bonsai has swept this country. In fact, while keeping the time-honored traditions and techniques, enterprising American growers have applied them to hundreds of new and different plants, even in fluorescent-light gardens. For material in this section I am indebted to Henry M. Cathey, head of ornamentals research for the U.S. Department of Agriculture. In fact, a bulletin prepared under his direction, called *Growing Bonsai*, makes an excellent introduction to the art; it is available for 35¢ from the Superintendent of Documents, U.S. Government Printing Office, Washington, D.C. 20402. Request Home and Garden Bulletin No. 206.

Dr. Cathey writes: "The aim of bonsai culture is to develop a tiny tree that has all the elements of a large tree growing in a natural setting. This look is achieved, principally, by branch and root pruning and shaping. Bonsai require daily watering during their growing season, and, because the plants are rooted in shallow pots, careful pruning.

"Bonsai are kept outdoors most of the year, but from time to time these miniaturized versions of nature are brought indoors for display. Only certain tropical trees, shrubs and vines can be kept continuously indoors as bonsai.

"Not all plants are equally effective as bonsai. To produce a realistic illusion of a mature tree, look for plants with these characteristics:

ABOVE: *Japanese maples trained as bonsai.*
BELOW: *Long-needled pine makes picturesque bonsai.*

- Small leaves or needles
- Short internodes or distances between leaves
- Attractive bark or surface roots
- Branching characteristics for good twig forms

"All parts of the ideal bonsai—trunk, branches, twigs, leaves, flowers, fruits, buds, roots—should be in perfect scale with the size of the tree. Plants used for bonsai should have small leaves, or leaves that become small under bonsai culture. Plants with overly large leaves such as the avocado will look out of proportion if chosen for bonsai. Among the plants with suitable small leaves and needles are spruce, pine, zelkova, pomegranate and certain oaks and maples."

Among the houseplants suited to bonsai culture, Dr. Cathey suggests woody types native to the tropics and subtropics of the world. These include: *Acacia baileyana,* aralia (*Polyscias* species *balfouriana, fruticosa* and *guilfoylei*), bird's-eye bush (*Ochna multiflora*), camellia, *Gardenia jasminoides radicans, Citrus* species (calamondin, kumquat, lemon, lime, orange and tangerine), *Eugenia uniflora,* Arizona and Monterey cypresses, *Ficus diversifolia, Cuphea hypssopifolia, Hibiscus rosa-sinensis cooperi, Malpighia coccigera, Jacaranda acutifolia, Crassula arguetea* (jade plant), *Jasminum parkeri, Murraea exotica, Trachelospermum jasminoides, Ficus retusa, Myrtus communis, Quercus suber, Nicodemia diversifolia, Grevillea robusta, Bauhinia variegata, Olea europaea, Oxera pulchella, Schinus molle, Pistacia chinensis, Carissa grandiflora, Delonix regia,* dwarf pomegranate, *Leucaena glauca, Calliandra surinamensis, Serissa foetida* and *Cassia eremophila.*

In addition to nursery stock, plants for bonsai can be collected from the wild or propagated from plants in your garden. You can also purchase trained bonsai plants in this country or import them from Japan (but only deciduous varieties ship well).

Dr. Cathey advises that the best method for a beginner to obtain bonsai is to buy nursery stock and develop his own:

These plants come in 1- to 5-gallon cans and their root systems have become adapted to cramped conditions.

Buy only young, healthy plants when purchasing nursery stock. Look for plants that are well rooted and well branched. Inspect the overall plant and then push back the foliage and examine the base from all sides. See if the foliage is full enough to be shaped into an interesting bonsai. Check to see if branches are where you will need them.

Do not thin the root system excessively all at once when placing the plant in a smaller container. By thinning the roots gradually and reducing the root system safely over a period of years, you will not damage the plant. If you prune and shape first and neglect thinning the roots, some plants may die.

Strive for flowing form when shaping bonsai. Visualize the overall theme and try to get a three-dimensional effect. Remember to select the front, back and sides of your bonsai before pruning, and don't forget to examine the roots that will influence the growth of these areas.

Use your pruning shears judiciously to make changes that benefit your bonsai. Fine adjustments are made by wiring and bending and thinning (removal of branches).

Before shaping a plant into a bonsai, decide whether the best attitude of the tree is upright, slanted, cascaded or semi-cascaded. Examine the general form of the tree and note whether it is straight or twisted. Match the potential of a tree to the style that fits it best. Decide whether the base will rise from the soil level or whether you will expose some bare roots.

You will need the following basic tools: a pair of sharp hook-and-blade pruning shears; a garden trowel; blunt sticks; a pair of sturdy wire cutters; copper wire of various lengths; and a sprinkling can. Also useful are scissors for trimming leaves, tweezers for nipping and brushes for cleaning the top soil.

Nursery plants are often overgrown and need much pruning to establish their best form. Through pruning you control growth and form by removing excess foliage and ugly limbs.

When pruning make all cuts above a bud, a side branch, or a main fork of the tree. Remove all buds except those on the outside of the trunk to force the growth outward and upward. Leave stubs flush with stem; long stubs serve

as an entry for insects (and besides, they are ugly). Avoid cutting back so far that you weaken the main branches.

When pruning, keep branches growing toward an open space instead of toward each other or the trunk. Do not shear bonsai as you would cut a hedge.

After deciding on the foliage form for your bonsai, remove all crossed branches and any dead branches. Then thin other branches until the tree takes on the form you have selected.

If you want to slant a tree that has been growing in an upright position and insure that branches take a normal shape, prune it in an upright attitude, and then tip it to where it should be and work on it that way.

Next, cut back new growth and thin out excess branches. When pruning an upright style, remove unneeded side branches and leave the center ones that will fill out as they grow.

A tree usually requires only one heavy pruning in its life to establish its basic form. After this initial pruning, shaping is done by nipping or pinching back to shape and develop the trunk and to control the overall size of the plant. Nipping controls new growth before it becomes so dense that it must be pruned.

Nipping is done not only to shape a plant but to develop more luxuriant foliage. As the new growth tips show up, nip them with your fingers, twisting rather than cutting or pulling. Also nip off tiny spurs that appear on the trunk or along heavy branches. These may develop into unsightly suckers that will leave scars when removed. Do not overdo this removal; be careful not to damage the foliage you leave on the plant.

After the top of a bonsai is pruned, trim the roots. Try to keep all fibrous roots and maintain a balance, if possible, of one branch for one root. Remove any roots that were damaged in digging. Leave the surface root system intact and make it appear as if the roots cling to the soil surface. Prune roots with sharp, sloping cuts to avoid damaging them.

The wiring and bending of branches that give bonsai its shape is unique to the art. Wiring is done after pruning when the tree has been thinned to essential branches.

Copper wire is usually used for shaping bonsai because it is flexible. The sizes of copper wire that are best for bonsai work are: 10, 12, 14, 16 and 18. Wire as light as No. 16 should be used for very thin branches and for tying rather than bending.

Wire evergreen trees only during their dormant period when the branches can be shaped without damaging growth. Wire deciduous trees only during their growing season.

The day before you wire a plant, do not water it; this will make the branches more flexible. Once a branch has taken on its trained form, remove the wire, straighten out its twists and flatten it with a mallet for reuse.

Wiring and shaping should begin at the lowest point on the tree, working upward. Do the following when wiring:

1. Anchor the end of the wire at the base of the tree before winding it. Push the end of the wire deep into the soil.

2. Wire from the trunk to the main branch. Use a foam pad under the wire to prevent damaging the bark. Keep the turns about 1/4 inch apart and spiral upward at a 45-degree angle. Do not wire too tightly, and do not damage leaves or stems.

After wiring, the plant is shaped or bent by hand. The trunk and main branches are gradually bent in the planned direction. Never try to straighten a branch that has been bent; this may split the bark.

Branches sometimes snap, even when carefully wired and bent. If the branch is not completely broken rejoin the broken ends, and wind some garden tape around the break. These fractures often heal quickly. If a branch snaps off, prune back cleanly at the first side branch.

Wire should be kept on the plant for not more than one year. Remove the wire before the bark becomes constricted; ridges will form if the wire is left on too long. When removing a wire, start at the outermost end of branches, and take care not to harm leaves, twigs or bark.

Other Garden Art Forms

If the idea of training a plant appeals to you, consider the techniques of topiary and espalier.

Classic topiary is represented by great old specimens of boxwood or privet artfully pruned into squares, balls, spirals, even animal and human forms. Today it is possible to buy ready-made topiary frames or armatures and with these you can have a lot of fun creating almost "instant" specimens by using small-leaved varieties of English ivy, creeping fig or any other vining or trailing plant. Three-dimensional forms are usually first filled and stuffed with unmilled sphagnum moss that has been soaked in water to which

LEFT: Small-flowered chrysanthemums may be trained as standards like this one. They can also be espaliered or trained into magnificent cascades. The secret lies in starting the training process early in the season and continuing until the flowers open. Never allow the soil to dry out.

ABOVE: Stylish topiaries like these two privets growing in Versailles tubs can be cultivated indoors or outdoors in large or small sizes, depending on the plant materials used and the shape desired.

RIGHT: To make a bromeliad tree you will need a good-sized piece of driftwood anchored in plaster of Paris. Wrap roots of assorted bromeliads in moist sphagnum moss, then tie securely into the crotches formed by the driftwood branches. Keep bromeliads happy by misting frequently with water.

fertilizer has been added. Then rooted cuttings of the selected plant are positioned as thickly as possible over the form.

A two-dimensional form for a topiary—for example, a wire coat hanger bent into a circle and anchored in a pot of soil—is in effect also a form for espaliering a plant. If you anchor that circle in the center of a pot filled with a long-stranded small-leaved English ivy, you can immediately tie it around the wire. Nip off wayward branches. Continue nipping and shaping in order to maintain a tidy, well-defined shape. By using galvanized wire or strips of redwood, you can create longer-lasting espalier frames in any pattern or design that pleases you, for example, classic trelliswork or treillage, a single trunk with one or more "U" shapes above it—in a stylized, flattened tree.

For containerized espaliers, you can use any of the tropical and subtropical plants suggested earlier in this chapter for bonsai training. Vines such as passiflora, clematis and dipladenia can also be trained in this manner.

11
Calendar Planting Guide for Tender Flowering Plants

NOTE: The temperature following the name of each plant suggests optimum nighttime temperature indoors during that part of the year when artificial heat is used. Most plants will adapt several—if not many—degrees above or below this optimum.

As these are tender plants—of tropical or semitropical origin—their time of flowering in the United States indoors or outdoors is often a mystery to the gardener.

January

BROWALLIA—65°—For plants to use outdoors in the spring and summer, start seeds now. They will grow slowly the first two months. Tip cuttings made now or in February will also provide flowering plants for spring planting out of doors.

CALENDULA—40°—Sow seeds now for May-to-hot-weather flowers. Varieties recommended include Sensation, Lemon King Select, Ball Orange Improved and Ball Gold. A sunny, cool, airy atmosphere is needed by calendulas.

CLERODENDRUM—60°—Now is the time to take 6-inch cuttings of half-ripened wood in order to have vigorous young plants of flowering size the coming season. Few flowers equal the fragrance of *C. fragrans pleniflorum.* The bleeding-heart vine (*C. thomsonae*) is a shrubby vine easily kept in bounds as a container plant. Trim back and repot old clerodendrum plants now.

DIDISCUS—50°—For blue-lace flowers beginning in April, sow seeds now in a 5-inch-deep flat. Thin to stand about 3 inches apart. Discard at the end of the flowering season.

FELICIA—50°—The blue daisy flowers of this plant (sometimes called agathea) are always welcome. Sow seeds now for blooming plants next winter. Pinch back several times until September to encourage branching.

GERANIUM—55°—Bedding plants cut back and brought in last fall can take a little more water as the days get longer. Feed lightly every two weeks. Cuttings of half-ripened wood made now will make excellent planting-out material next spring. Try some of the new seed-grown geranium varieties.

GYPSOPHILA—60°—Sow seeds of baby's-breath now in deep flats, or an 8-inch standard flowerpot. Be sure to purchase seeds of the annual type so you will have flowers this year.

IMPATIENS—60°—Sow seeds now for an abundance of flowering plants at planting-out time this spring. There's a wealth of beauty in the new dwarf impatiens hybrids. Check your seed catalog for descriptions. For full shade to semishade indoors or outdoors, few plants can equal the flower crop given by impatiens. If you have old plants of favorite impatiens, tip cuttings can be started now.

LOBELIA—55°—For baskets, window boxes, edging and pots, it's hard to have enough lobelia plants. Start seeds now indoors so the plants will be blooming at planting-out time. Even if summer heat takes its toll of these cool-loving plants, you'll still reap a big flower show early in the season if you start seeds now.

MARIGOLD—55°—Most of today's hybrids will bloom in about 90 days from seeds. The Spun Gold and Spun Yellow types are especially nice for a bold block of color in a sunny place indoors during April and May; then you can transplant them outdoors.

SALPIGLOSSIS — 55° — These fascinating plants with spectacular trumpet flowers need an early start. Sow seeds now; transplant later to individual 3-inch pots if you plan to put them outdoors after frost danger is past. If you have a greenhouse, transplant three seedlings to each 8- or 10-inch pot. Stake and tie as necessary.

SCHIZANTHUS—55°—Sow seeds now for a late-spring-into-summer showing of butterfly flowers. Transplant first to 3-inch pots, then finish at a 6-inch size. Pinch twice to induce branching. I transplant three seedlings to each 3-inch pot. Two of these I pinch, one I don't. The one not pinched blooms earlier than the other two, thus providing a longer season. The same technique will work with other plants that get pinched—snapdragons, for example.

February

ABUTILON—60°—If you have established flowering maples, now would be a good time to repot. Trim back branches that are too long, or which make the plant unshapely. Trimmings may be rooted to have compact, flowering plants for indoors, or you can use these outdoors this spring. For "wow-some" large-size flowers in rich colors—varying from yellow and orange to dark red, paling to pink—plant seeds of Thompson and Morgan's Large-Flowered Mixed hybrids. Sown in January or February, they will start flowering about the end of July. By pinching out the leading shoot, their height can be kept to about 18 inches.

ACALYPHA—60°—Now is the time to root 4-inch tip cuttings of the chenille plant, as well as the variety called "copper leaf." Root in a warm, moist place; provide high humidity and keep shaded until rooting occurs.

ACHIMENES—60°—Now is the time to plant the scaly rhizomes of this popular summer-blooming gesneriad, a relative of the African violet and gloxinia. Six rhizomes will make a big show in a 6-inch pot. Warmth, high humidity and evenly moist growing medium will encourage rapid growth, with flowers beginning in late spring. If you have a greenhouse going in summer, achimenes can be the stars of the show. Outdoors in warm weather, they are as desirable for shady gardens as impatiens.

AGAPANTHUS—45°—Now is a good time to divide and repot large, crowded specimens. To grow a plentiful supply of this "lily of the Nile," sow seeds in a warm, moist place. First blooms can be expected in three years.

BEGONIA—65°—Divide, cut back and repot large wax or semperflorens begonias. If you take cuttings, make them of base growth that shows an indication of branching. Cuttings made from vigorous tip growth often root poorly if at all, and then they may not branch properly. There's still time to sow seeds, too, for flowering plants next summer, and real specimens next fall and winter. Try some of the newest dwarf hybrids, but also try Red and Rose Butterfly—magnificent new semperflorens with flowers to 2½ inches across! At a short distance away these appear to be tuberous begonias.

CALADIUM—60°—For specimen plants in full foliage by June, start the tubers now in warmth and moisture. You can start a quantity of tubers in a deep flat of vermiculite, transplanting later to individual 6- to 8-inch pots. Or start individual tubers in 6-inch pots. Planting caladium tubers upside down results in more shoots, and thus more but smaller leaves.

CAMPANULA—45°—Make cuttings now of C. isophylla and similar types in order to have a plentiful supply of blooming plants next fall. Keep warm, moist and in high humidity, with shade, while roots are forming.

CESTRUM—60°—If you like fragrant flowers, try some of the cestrums. C. noc-turnum is the plant I grow for its creamy white flowers that give off a fragrance like Chanel No. 5 every evening in the summer. If you have a cestrum already, now is the time to root 3-inch tip cuttings.

COLEUS—60°—This month take 3-inch tip cuttings of your favorite plants. Sow seeds of selected strains, or named varieties, in order to have an abundance of plants this spring. Check every coleus plant in your collection for signs of mealybug infestation. Coleus and mealybugs have such an affinity for each other, if you find them together, discard both. Start over with seeds.

FREESIA—65-70°—Sow seeds now, of an outstanding strain like Super Giant Hybrids Mixed, for flowers next fall. Once germinated no extra warmth is needed —they'll do better in a range of 50-60°. Move outdoors for the summer, but provide plenty of water and fertilize every other week. Bring inside in September.

GERBERA—70°—Sow seeds now in warmth in order to have vigorous, young, flowering plants for next fall. Thompson and Morgan's Florists Strain Mixed will open flowers measuring to 5 inches in diameter with broad, stiff petals, and long, strong stems.

LANTANA—55°—Make 3-inch cuttings of older plants in order to have plenty of material for planting-out next spring.

TUBEROUS BEGONIA—65°—Start tubers now in order to have flowering plants by early summer. They need a warm, moist situation. Moist, shredded redwood bark makes an excellent starting medium, or you can use the time-honored vermiculite, or 50-50 mixture of peat moss and sand.

TULBAGHIA—50°—Now is the time to divide and repot this intermittent-blooming bulbous plant. It's always nice to propagate an unusual but easy-to-grow plant like tulbaghia in order to have extra plants to pass along to gardening friends.

VERBENA—50°—Start seeds now in order to have flowering plants by planting-out time this spring. This tender perennial, which we cultivate as a hardy annual, doesn't bloom as quickly from seed as some common annuals, and your garden will benefit from giving it an early start in the greenhouse.

March

ALLAMANDA—60°—Take cuttings of last year's growth and root in a warm, moist, shaded place. Vermiculite makes an excellent rooting medium.

APHELANDRA — 55° — Now is the time to take tip cuttings of this handsome foliage plant. Root as described for allamanda. Young plants are compact and usually attractive—nice to present as gifts.

ARDISIA—60°—The coralberry comes in for all kinds of attention this month: established plants may be repotted. It's also the time to sow seeds or plant cuttings in moist soil and warmth.

AZALEA—55°—On the surface of a mixture of peat moss and sand, sow seeds of a good hybrid strain of azaleas this month. Be sure the medium never dries out. If water in your area is on the alkaline side, water from time to time with an acid-type fertilizer of special azalea food.

BELOPERONE—55°—There's still time to take tip cuttings of the shrimp plant and place in individual small pots of moist rooting medium in order to have plenty for outdoor planting this summer.

BOUVARDIA—60°—Plant tip cuttings now in moist rooting medium in order to have vigorous, young plants next fall.

FREESIA—45°—For real abundance, sow hybrid seeds now. Plant in a wooden flat at least 6 inches deep. Keep in constant growth, right through the usual dormant time of summer and early fall. This means the soil should never dry out and that feeding needs to be kept up until blooming begins around Christmas.

GYPSOPHILA—60°—To catch a quick crop of annual baby's-breath before summer, sow seeds now. You will have cutting material in about eight weeks, perfect filler for early spring bouquets, not to mention the pleasure of the flowers for your container garden.

KAEMPFERIA—60°—If you want flowers indoors this summer, start some kaempferias or ginger-lilies now. Mail-order specialists stock them.

PRIMULA—45-50°—Now is the time to start seeds of the showy frost-tender primroses—*P. sinensis, P. malacoides* and *P. obconica*—in order to have flowering specimens of outstanding size next winter and spring. Seeds germinate well at 60 degrees. When large enough to transplant, move to community pots or flats, transplanting later to individual 4's or 5's, finally to 6- and 7-inch pots in early fall.

ZANTEDESCHIA—55°—Now is the time to plant tubers of pink and yellow calla-lilies, as well as the newer Sunrise Hybrids which come in many interesting shades. Three tubers to a 10-inch pot will provide quite an attractive specimen by midsummer. Keep warm and just moist until growth begins, then pour on the water and begin biweekly feeding after foliage growth is apparent.

April

BEGONIA, TUBEROUS—65°—Plant dormant tubers now, keeping barely moist, but nicely warm, until root growth is apparent, then provide more moisture as leaves begin to grow.

BOUGAINVILLEA—55°—Make tip cuttings 3 or 4 inches long and root in a warm, moist, shaded place. As new growth begins to be vigorous, pinch out the growing tips to induce branching. Continue this practice through summer and early fall. Once well-rooted, new plants can take full sun. The effects of this baking through the summer season seem to bring on all the more bloom the following fall and winter.

CHRYSANTHEMUM—60°—If mums are in your plans for late summer, fall and early winter color in containers, begin today by writing for catalogs from specialists. There isn't a day to waste if you are to have time to study lists and descriptions before sending your order for rooted cuttings. In the best catalogs you will find French imports, anemone and spoon types, spider and threadlike varieties, cushions, pompons, buttons, tree-forming, cascades and football types.

CROTON—Tip cuttings 5 or 6 inches long may be rooted now in warmth (75-80°) and high humidity, using a porous rooting medium kept moist (equal parts vermiculite and peat moss may be used). Today's croton varieties make unusually showy foliage plants indoors and out. Direct sun is not needed—only bright diffused light will bring on the characteristic foliage coloration.

HIBISCUS, CHINESE—65°—Now is the time to take 4-inch stem cuttings in order to have plenty of vigorous, young plants coming on. Since these bloom on new wood, it is not unusual for cuttings in the rooting medium to provide an occasional bloom.

MARGUERITE—50°—Boston or Paris daisies known botanically as *Chrysanthemum frutescens,* are great to have, both in the house or greenhouse and later outdoors in the summer. Now is the time to start 3-inch tip cuttings in order to have bushy, well-formed plants for flowering next winter and spring. You can buy pink, white or yellow varieties. For best effect, plant three or four rooted cuttings of each color to an 8-inch pot.

PENTAS—50°—This everblooming plant is useful not only in the house (stake for upright growth, or let it billow out of a basket) but also for bedding outdoors in the summer. Before you put stock plants outdoors, take 3-inch tip cuttings. Root in moist vermiculite at about 70° in a humid, shady place. These young plants, if kept pinched during the summer, will be ready to put on a real flower show indoors next fall.

May

AFRICAN VIOLET—65°—Sow seeds now in order to have flowering-size plants next winter and spring. Park's Sure-Fire starting mix makes an excellent medium on which to sow the fine seeds (they need not be covered with it, but merely pressed lightly into the surface), or you can use finely milled sphagnum moss. This is also the season to divide multiple-crowned plants, and an excellent time to order new kinds.

ANEMONE — 40° — Plant seeds of hybrid strains now for flowers of unusually good quality next winter. Protection from burning sun, evenly moist soil, and as much coolness as possible are the rules for taking the seedlings through summer. Transplanting to 4-inch pots will need to be done by September.

CINERARIA—45°—Sow seeds now in order to have plants of specimen size that bloom next winter and spring. It's important with cinerarias to keep the seedlings growing without check. This means transplanting regularly so that roots do not become potpound; feeding biweekly; keeping the soil moist at all times; and spraying as necessary to prevent aphids from damaging new growth.

CITRUS—50°—If you have any of the dwarf citrus in your collection, now is the time to make tip cuttings of half-ripened wood. Once rooted these young plants will begin to bloom and bear fruit; these make excellent gifts. Cuttings need shade and high humidity while roots form.

FELICIA—50°—Sow seeds now of this blue-flowered daisy, often called "agathea." Flowers will come next winter and spring. Seedlings need lots of fresh air in the summer, and plenty of sunlight, combined with regular pinching of tip growth. If you have established plants, now is the time to root tip cuttings in moist vermiculite.

GERANIUM—55°—Take cuttings now in order to have plenty of pot-size flowering specimens for next winter and spring indoors. This is also the time to start training a strongly upright-growing geranium to standard or tree form. Pinch or rub out all sideshoots as quickly as they can be seen. Provide a sturdy stake at the beginning, one of the height you wish the tree to be. When the tip of the geranium reaches this height, pinch it out to start the branching process. As each new branch reaches a length of 2 to 3 inches, pinch out the tip until a well-branched head is achieved.

HOYA—60°—Now is the time to root cuttings of the wax plant in moist vermiculite; provide warmth, humidity and shade until rooting occurs. Look in catalogs of houseplant specialists for new and unusual kinds of hoyas.

TIBOUCHINA—55°—This purple-flowered plant makes an excellent container subject for spring-to-fall bloom. Now is the time to make 3-inch tip cuttings; root in moist vermiculite in a shaded, moist and warm situation. If you want the cutting to grow into a bushy, compact plant, pinch out growing tips several times, up to September. If you want to develop a tree or standard shape, follow instructions given this month for geraniums.

June

ACACIA—40°—If you have a cool greenhouse or sun porch in winter and spring, acacias should play a big role in the February-to-April flower show. Cuttings made now will root in a mixture of peat moss and sand; keep evenly moist. Acacias need to be summered outdoors in a cool, partially shaded situation. Avoid dry heat at any time.

ACALYPHA—60°—The popular "chenille plant," "copper leaf" and other acalyphas make showy plants for any container garden. There are new kinds coming onto the market, especially through commercial greenhouses; keep an eye out for these when you visit your florist. Four-inch tip cuttings root readily now in moist vermiculite; provide a humid, shaded, warm place. The chenille plant (*A. hispida*) is especially valuable for fall-to-spring flowers which may vary from rosy to rusty red, to the pinkish hues of *A. h. alba* strains.

AZALEA—55°—For fall and winter flowers in a moderately cool place, hardly any plant rivals today's azaleas. It's always a wise investment to buy a heavily budded plant at your local florists in November, but you can also have fun propagating favorite plants from 3-inch tip cuttings made in the summer; root in an evenly moist mixture of peat moss and sand in a situation that has good light (but no direct sun) and high humidity.

CALCEOLARIA—45°—Start seeds now as cool as possible (50° is ideal) in order to have flower-covered plants next winter and spring. Calceolarias need a sunny, moist, airy and cool atmosphere —a combination difficult to provide in many areas during the summer. Protection from midday summer sun is a necessity. Routine care is very much like that for cinerarias (see under May notes).

CYCLAMEN—50°—Now is the time to start seeds in a moist mixture of peat moss and sand in order to have flowering-size seedlings about 18 months from now. Nearly every gardener knows what a pleasure it is to have a flower-covered and bud-filled cyclamen from the florist, but real happiness to anyone who admires these plants is to grow a quantity from seeds.

EXACUM—50°—Start seeds now of this lavender-blue, starry flower for a showing this coming winter. It's important to keep the seedlings evenly moist at all times and to provide protection from burning summer sun. Otherwise this biennial is easily cultivated and worth starting each June.

MYOSOTIS—50°—Start seeds now of 'Blue Bird' or 'Christmas Bouquet' for forget-me-nots beginning this December and continuing into next spring. This summer it will be necessary to provide a place that's moist, as cool as possible, and partially shaded. By autumn transplant to individual 5-inch pots, or three to an 8-inch container.

PASSIFLORA—50°—Tip cuttings 4 to 6 inches long root easily now in moist vermiculite; keep warm and shaded. Kinds recommended for containers include *P. alato-caerulea* (unusual flowers combining the colors blue, pink, purple and white) and scarlet-flowered *P. coccinea.* Either type can be trained upward on a small trellis.

PRIMULA—45°—Sow seeds now of *P. malacoides* and *P. obconica.* The rule for success is to provide 60-degree temperatures during the germination period, and then ample shading and cooling through hot weather. By early fall individual seedlings will need 5-inch pots, and later the largest ones can be put into 7- or 8-inch pots.

PUNICA — 55° — The dwarf pomegranate makes an excellent houseplant, and now is the time to root cuttings of half-ripened wood. Plant in moist vermiculite and keep shaded and moist. This is one plant that doesn't mind summertime sun and warmth, provided the soil is kept moist. If you enjoy training plants, here's an excellent subject for bonsai work.

July

CELOSIA—55–60°—*C. plumosa,* the plume cockscomb, has been vastly improved in recent years. Heights range from 8 inches to several feet; colors have all the brilliancy of autumn leaves. For pots of this color indoors in autumn, select types that grow not more than 15 inches tall. Sow seeds now on the surface of a pot of moist vermiculite. Cover lightly. Keep moist. After germination, feed lightly with every watering. Transplant to 3-inch pots of soil (equal parts peat, garden loam, sand). Keep seedlings outdoors until late August or early September. Move to 5- or 6-inch pots when roots begin to fill the 3's. Continue feeding. By October these July-started seeds will have turned into striking specimens, a marvelous foil for any chrysanthemum show. They'll remain attractive at least until after the holidays.

CROSSANDRA—55–68°—Three-inch tip cuttings root easily now in moist potting soil, warmth and high humidity. It's a small-growing plant with glossy, dark green leaves and a nearly endless show of salmon-orange flowers. Great to grow in a fluorescent-light garden.

DIMORPHOTHECA—50-65°—This low-growing African daisy flower needs all the sun you can provide in winter. Sow seeds now for blooms beginning in four to five months.

FUCHSIA—55-60°—Root cuttings now to have vigorous young plants for next spring and summer. These will be ready for 5-inch pots next March.

HELIOTROPE — 60° — Make cuttings now from selected specimens growing outdoors.

NERIUM—45-55°—Root cuttings now for vigorous young plants next year of oleander. 'Mrs. Roeding' blooms longest.

NICOTIANA—50-60°—Sow seeds now for winter and spring blooms from the flowering tobacco. Old-fashioned white has fragrance at night. Compact 'White Bedder' is best for potting.

OSMANTHUS—50°—Insert 3-inch tip cuttings in moist peat and sand; provide shade and high humidity. The white, wonderfully fragrant flowers appear almost year round.

PANSY—40-50°—Sow seeds of a winter-blooming type now. Keep constantly moist and as cool as possible.

SNAPDRAGON—45-60°—Sow seeds now for December bloom. Grow single stem for earlier bloom; or, at 6- to 8-inch height, pinch back to three sets of leaves, to obtain more but later bloom.

August

AGERATUM—55°—Sow seeds now for winter-spring bloom. New 'Blue Blazer' is highly recommended. Cuttings made now of plants growing in the garden will bloom indoors beginning in autumn.

BELLIS—45-50°—Sow seeds now for English daisy flowers of pink, rose or white next winter and spring. Provide sunny, airy, moist atmosphere.

CALENDULA—45-55°—Sow seeds now for October to January bloom in various shades of orange to yellow to palest cream. Best for pot culture: 'Sensation,' 'Lemon King Select,' 'Ball Orange Improved' and 'Ball Gold.'

CALLA, WHITE — 60-65° — Plant roots now for white, fragrant flowers next winter and spring; one to a 6-inch pot, three to a 10-inch tub.

CAMELLIA—45-65°—Now is the time to make tip cuttings of half-ripened wood. Insert in mixture of moist peat and sand. Provide shade and high humidity.

CENTAUREA—45-55°—Seeds of bachelor's-buttons sown now will give welcome winter flowers. 'Dwarf Blue Boy' is a good choice, although hybrid mixtures offer an interesting color range. A cool, moist, airy atmosphere during fall and winter will help prevent red spider-mite attacks.

CINERARIA—45-55°—Sow seeds in a cool, moist, shaded place early this month for blooms next spring. In autumn transplant to small pots. Keep moist at all times. Move on to 5- or 6-inch pots by January. Spray to control aphids.

CYRTANTHUS—50-65°—Now is the time to order and plant bulbs of this easily grown little amaryllid for fall and winter blooms. Amaryllis culture.

FREESIA—50°—Make first planting of these corms (six to a 6-inch pot) by the end of the month. Continue planting every two or three weeks until December 1. Corms planted now will yield late December and January bloom.

LACHENALIA—50°—Freesia culture will do nicely for the Cape cowslip which yields red or yellow flowers from early winter until spring. Plant six corms to a 6-inch pot in August.

MARIGOLD—50-60°—Sow seeds now for winter and spring bloom. Dwarf French types will do nicely in 3- and 4-inch pots; American hybrids may be finished in 6's. Large hybrids like 'Toreador' bloom in about three months from seed at 60-degree nighttime temperature.

NASTURTIUM—50°—For winter flowers, sow seeds now. The Gleam Hybrids are recommended; also some of the new dwarf hybrids. Try as basket plants for a refreshing change.

NEMESIA—45-50°— This cool-loving annual with brilliant flowers of blue, pink, red, rose, scarlet, orange and yellow, will give winter bloom from seeds started now. A cool, moist, airy atmosphere is the key to success.

September

AMARYLLIS — 60° — Order bulbs now of named Dutch, South African and American hybrids. There's much excitement to be found in hybrid amaryllis these days. Each bulb is a longtime investment in pleasure. Pot up with neck of the bulb exposed; keep moist and on the cool side while roots form.

ANEMONE—50°—Now is the time to order, and plant as quickly as possible, the clawlike roots of *Anemone coronaria* types. Instructions that come with them may advise to soak the roots 24 hours in water before planting. Unless you have been successful with this method in the past, we recommend that the roots simply be planted "claws" down, slightly covered and then that they be kept evenly moist in coolness (40-50°). Once well rooted, the pots of anemones can then be moved to the light for growing on. Be sure that anemones do not dry out severely at any time after growth begins. Also, keep an eye out for green aphids; they often cluster on new leaves and buds.

GLOXINIA—60°—Sow seeds now of hybrid strains, such as Buell, in order to have a glorious showing of flowering plants next March, April and May. The seeds

need a warm, moist, humid place in which to start. Seedlings started now will have nice-sized tubers formed by next summer, at which time the plants may be dried off and rested. Start the year-old tubers into new growth in October for another spring flower show the following year. Repeat this cycle over and over.

IXIA—55°—This member of the iris family, and the similar sparaxis, should be much more commonly cultivated. Pot six corms to a 6-inch pot. Keep around 40 to 50 degrees and evenly moist until rooting is well along. Then begin forcing in a sunny, airy, moist environment.

LACHENALIA — 50° — This bulb flower is commonly known as the Cape cowslip. Culture is practically identical to that described this month for ixia. After flowering, the rule is to rest the bulbs nearly dry and moderately warm until replanting time in early fall.

ORNITHOGALUM—55°—Essentially, culture for this bulb flower is the same as that outlined here for ixia and lachenalia, except you will need only three bulbs for a 6-inch pot. These plants need some staking as growth progresses.

SCHIZANTHUS — 55° — The poor-man's orchid, or butterfly flower, is an easily cultivated annual that gives a lot of color from airy, graceful flowers in spring. Seeds sown now will yield late winter and spring blooms. Pinch once or twice to encourage bushiness.

October

ASTER, CHINA—55°—Seeds started now will provide welcome flowers from winter until mid-spring. The seedlings will need four hours supplementary light every evening from the time they are in seedflats until buds are beginning to open.

CALENDULA — 50° — This easy annual, known to herb growers as the "pot uary. You may select from several flower colors and types. Colors are welcome and cheerful in the winter: lemony yellow, golden yellow and glowing gold. Abundant sunlight in an airy, cool, moist atmosphere keeps calendula growth compact; keep soil evenly moist at all times.

CROCUS—50°—Pot up several containers of crocus corms now to force into bloom beginning after the holidays. Keep moist, cool and dark while roots form. Then, bring to a light spot for forcing. Other "little" bulbs are equally interesting as forcing material: muscari, chionodoxa, scilla and eranthis.

CYRTANTHUS — 55° — This small-growing relative of the amaryllis makes a delightful addition to any collection. The flowers come off and on over a long period beginning at the holidays and continuing until spring. Culture is the same as for hybrid amaryllis: start into growth in autumn, water and feed through winter, spring and early summer, then dry off and rest in late summer and early fall.

DAFFODIL—50°—If you follow some very simple rules, the only mistake you can make with daffodils is to not force enough. Pot up as early as you can get the bulbs, grouping them in pots of a size that will be convenient for you to handle. Personally I prefer large bulb pans that will accommodate at least six, and preferably a dozen bulbs. Keep moist, cool and dark while roots form. After eight weeks, you may check for root growth, and if found to be extensive, forcing may begin in an airy, moist, light atmosphere.

HYACINTH—50°—Forcing is virtually the same as for daffodils, except hyacinths tend to be easier and more tolerant of varied temperatures. Even one bulb forced in a 3-inch pot makes quite a fragrant display. The Roman types planted now will give bloom for the holi-

days. The Dutch hybrids started now may be forced into bloom as early as January.

PAPERWHITE NARCISSUS—55°—These popular bulbs are probably the easiest of all bulb flowers for forcing into bloom. Buy as many as you can possibly afford because there never seem to be enough pots. I force one pot a week as long as they last. The fragrant white or golden blooms are tremendously welcome in the middle of winter. Nestle the bulbs in moist soil; keep cool, moist and dark while roots form. Then bring to light for forcing, which takes about four weeks.

STOCK—55°—These fragrant flowers are among the most easily cultivated of all container annuals. Sow seeds now for late winter and spring bloom. Provide ample room for the roots to grow, and feed biweekly after New Year's. A sunny, airy, moist, cool atmosphere is the key to large flower spikes; staking may be needed, also.

SWEET PEA—45°—Sow seeds now for midwinter to spring flowers. The All-America Selections winner Knee-Hi 'San Francisco' makes an excellent choice. 'Bijou' is also a well-behaved type for container culture.

TULIP—50°—Forcing of these bulb flowers is about the same as for daffodils, except they often get a severe attack of bulb aphids, and require careful spraying or dipping with a pesticide to prevent damage to the flowers. The single- and double-flowered early types are by far the best for forcing.

November

CHRISTMAS CACTUS—60°—Remember that this is a short-day plant which needs the naturally short days of autumn in order to bloom. If you work in the same room at night, turn a cardboard carton over your Christmas cactus before you turn the lights on. It is important also to keep the soil a little less moist at this time of the year; increase the water supply in late winter or early spring.

CLEMATIS—55°—Now's the time to buy hybrid clematis, in dormancy, and start them into growth for winter-spring bloom. Pot up in a 6- to 8-inch container, depending on the size of the root ball. Use a mixture of equal parts garden loam, peat moss and sand, adding a tablespoon of ground limestone to each pot. A sunny, airy atmosphere will help bring on lush growth and the much-admired flowers.

POINSETTIA—60°—Here's another plant that needs short days in order to flower. Actually, the Christmas flower show traces back to late September and the month of October when short days are needed, but don't upset what has been started already by burning lights on your plants at night this month.

ROSES—55°—Dormant bushes available now offer all kinds of opportunity to the container gardener. Any hybrid tea, floribunda or grandiflora is worth trying for a season. You can transplant it later to the outdoor garden. Pot up dormant bushes now in a 12- to 18-inch container. Use a mixture of two parts garden loam, one part peat moss and one part sand. You can avoid problems of pest and disease by spraying on a regular basis with a rose pesticide. Another possibility for roses in containers lies in the miniatures—both bush and tree types.

December

CENTAUREA—50°—Of all the colorful annual flowers cultivated in pots, this is one of the easiest. Sow seeds now for spring flowers. Plenty of root-spreading room in evenly moist soil will keep the buds coming; and the more you cut, the more they'll bloom. Choose from the marvelous blues, or be adventuresome with the maroons, lavenders, rose-pinks and near-whites.

GLORIOSA-LILY — 60° — This climbing lily makes a spectacular showing for springtime, and now's the time to start the tubers. These may be 6 to 8 inches long, so that a sizable bulb pan is likely to be needed for planting. Provide a sunny, airy, moist atmosphere and something on which the tendril-tipped leaves can climb.

LOBELIA—60°—Now's the time to start seeds of this attractive plant for borders, baskets, benches and tubs. There are kingly purples, electric blues and snowy whites. This small-growing, tender perennial thrives in a sunny, airy, cool atmosphere.

NIEREMBERGIA—50°—Better known as cup flower, here's another subject for basketry and shelf work. It's a tender perennial that can be kept over year to year; the technique is to shear back to 3 or 4 inches after a period of heavy flowering. Seeds started now will give spring flowers.

PETUNIA—55°—For April flowers, now is the time to sow seeds of the fancy double grandifloras. The single types, too, offer a splash of color in return for very little trouble. They're especially enjoyable in baskets, or cascading from shelves. Plant breeders have spent as much time in recent years on the petunia as any other type plant; it's a good idea to cash in on the tremendous array of colors and forms available.

TUBEROUS BEGONIA—70°—These beautiful flowers are always photogenic, but they really have to be seen to be appreciated. There's no better way to see an abundance of them than to start hybrid seeds now. They're minute seeds, almost like a particle of dust, but growing them is fairly easy if you sow them on the surface of a moist, sterile medium such as Jiffy Mix or milled sphagnum moss. Seeds started now will yield flowering-size plants for next season.

12
Propagating Plants

Being a successful container gardener requires considerable experience, but the basics are quite simple. Each plant needs a suitable container and growing medium and thereafter light and water. Such amenities as feeding, providing more humidity in the atmosphere, and grooming can be developed as the need arises.

The essentials of potting and repotting, and starting container plants from seeds, cuttings, bulbs and transplants are covered in this chapter by photographs and captions. Study each set of these and you will be well on your way to understanding how all of these basics work together to make a successful container garden—and gardener.

Supplies needed for starting all kinds of seeds include, clockwise from upper left, milled sphagnum moss, vermiculite, charcoal chips, fiber flats, peat pots. Available locally and by mail from plant specialists.

ABOVE: Fill fiber flat with vermiculite.

ABOVE: Sow seeds in shallow drills; label each row.

ABOVE: Cover seeds lightly if packet so directs.

ABOVE: Moisten well with a gentle stream of water.

ABOVE: Enclose planting in plastic bag to keep moist.
BELOW: Transplant each seedling to a peat pot.

ABOVE: Transplant early before seedlings crowd.
BELOW: Healthy seedling ready for a larger pot.

ABOVE: Overgrown African violet ready for repotting.

ABOVE: Remove from pot; cut apart with a knife.

ABOVE: Plant yielded three divisions plus leaves.

ABOVE: Sink is convenient place for potting.

ABOVE: Transplants need to be well moistened.
BELOW: Root leaves in soil or water.

ABOVE: African violet leaves prepared for rooting.
BELOW: Some begonia leaves will also root.

ABOVE: *Tuberous begonia seedlings growing under lights.*

ABOVE: *Three-month-old tuberous begonia seedlings.*

ABOVE: *Gently firm soil about the roots of seedlings.*

ABOVE: *Planting tulip bulbs preparatory to forcing.*

ABOVE: *Leave neck of amaryllis bulb exposed.*
BELOW: *Surface roots indicate need for a larger pot.*

ABOVE: *Steven McDonald adds label to amaryllis.*
BELOW: *Using tepid, sudsy water to remove insects.*

13
Soils and
Other Growing Media

Container plants are presently cultivated in two basic growing mediums: (1) soil-based and (2) soil-less.

Soils

Soil-based planting mediums are mixed according to recipes. There are almost as many recipes for potted plants as there are pot gardeners. The basic, general-purpose potting soil is usually comprised of equal parts garden loam, sphagnum peat moss and clean sand (*not* sand from the beach). To amend this for desert cacti and other succulents you might mix one part garden loam, one part sphagnum peat moss and two parts clean sand. If you want to grow a jungle plant that needs lots of humus (for example, a philodendron or rex begonia) you could mix one part garden loam, one part clean sand and two parts sphagnum peat moss.

Where to obtain good garden loam can be quite a problem, especially if you live in a city apartment. Even if you have a vegetable or flower garden, the soil may not be all that good for container gardening. For one thing, soil used for pot plants ideally should be pasteurized first. This can be done by baking a container of soil for an hour at 150 to 180 degrees F.; moisten the soil well before baking; allow it to cool overnight before using in a planting mixture.

Packaged prepared potting soils are available wherever plants are sold. In my experience all of these are too heavy in texture. They should be mixed with peat moss, sand (or perlite, a sterile substitute for sand) or vermiculite (also a sterile medium which can be used in place of well-rotted leaf mold, an ingredient you may find listed in some potting-soil recipes). To mix a good general-purpose potting medium based on a packaged prepared potting soil, try combining equal parts of the soil, perlite, vermiculite and peat moss. This mixture will grow almost any container plant, indoors or outdoors.

Growing mediums based on soil will grow excellent plants in combination with normal feeding practices. On any container of garden fertilizer you will find instructions for how much and how often to feed. Follow these—but if you deviate, feed less, not more than the container recommends.

Soil-less

Soil-less growing mediums are based mostly on formulas perfected at Cornell University and the University of California. They are comprised of more or less sterile ingredients and require constant feeding for uniform growth. Most soil-less growers use a combination of organic fertilizers (fish emulsion, for example) and chemical fertilizers, feeding one time with one, the next with the other. For best results a little fertilizer should be applied every time the plant is watered. By a "little," I mean one-fourth to one-fifth the amount recommended on the fertilizer container for standard soil-grown pot plants. If the fertilizer manufacturer recommends the use of one teaspoon fertilizer to one quart of water, you would use a fourth of a teaspoon of fertilizer to one quart of water and apply this solution every time you water the plant growing in soil-less.

Soil-less planting mediums are sold under various trade names. These in-

Soil-less mixes are lightweight, even when moist.

clude Jiffy Mix, Redi-earth, Supersoil, Pro-mix, Vita-Bark University Mix and others.

Solving Plant Problems

There are almost countless problems that may be encountered in container gardening, yet almost all of them pertain to the simple basics of light, temperature, humidity, watering, feeding and a few pests. Diseases, for example, fungus or virus, are of no great threat to most container gardens. Symptoms and solutions for the most frequent problems follow.

Leaf tips and edges dry, brown, dead. Plant is too hot and dry at the same time. Keep soil evenly moist. Avoid drafts of hot, dry air from artificial heat. The plant may be receiving too much direct sun. Too much fertilizer might also cause this symptom.

Many leaves turn yellow and fall off within a short period of time. Change in environment. Lack of sufficient light. Overfeeding. Too hot and dry or too cold and wet at the same time. If leaves are yellow-flecked and tiny cobwebbing is found between leaf stems and main stalk, red spider-mites are probably present (see following paragraph).

Leaves yellow-flecked; cobwebs between leaf stems and main stalks. Red spider-mite is probably present. This pest thrives in stale, hot, dry air. Rinse the plant thoroughly in water of room temperature. Lower temperatures. Increase humidity. Add fresh air circulating among plants. Spray alternately, once a week, using Kelthane one week, Dimite the next, until no traces of red spider-mite can be seen when you examine growth through a magnifying glass.

New growth pale and weak. Lack of light. Temperatures too hot or too cold. The plant may also need to be fed.

No flowers. Lack of light. Too hot and

dry or too cold and wet at the same time. Too much nitrogen in the soil; change to a blossom-booster type fertilizer, commonly marketed specifically for African violets but also useful for promoting bloom on any indoor plant. If nonbloomer in question is sensitive to long or short days, this could be the problem. For example, chrysanthemums, Christmas cactus, poinsettias and kalanchoes bloom when the days are naturally short in autumn and early winter. If they receive any artificial light in the period between sundown and sunup in September and October, they will not bloom for the holidays. By contrast, long-day plants such as summer-flowering tuberous begonias and gloxinias will not bloom unless they have approximately 16 hours illumination in every 24. In the summertime this is no problem, but if you want winter bloom, supplementary fluorescent light will be required.

Plant parts coated with cottony white insects and matter. Mealybugs are present. Use spray or dip of malathion, having first washed off as much of the cottony residue as possible in tepid water to which a little household detergent has been added. A Shell No-Pest Strip placed in a room with houseplants will eradicate mealybugs, red spider-mites and other common pests. Each Strip is efficacious for up to four months and only one is needed in an average room.

Healthy plant suddenly wilts even though soil is moist. Overwatering or lack of drainage has caused roots to suffocate and rot. Take tip cuttings of remaining healthy growth; discard old plant.

Small brown "bumps" on leaves and stems. Brown scale is present. Remove each with tip of a pocketknife or with your fingernails. Use soft cotton cloth moistened in water to which a little household detergent has been added and wipe leaves and stems clean of all sticky residue left by the scale. If plant is too large to deal with by hand, spray with malathion or use a Shell No-Pest Strip in the same room.

Little white insects fly around plant when it is disturbed. White flies are the culprits. You'll find them clustered under the leaves. Frequent pest of container tomatoes, fuchsias and lantanas. If present on any vegetable or herb, use only a pesticide recommended for food crops (check labels at your local garden center; no recommendation is made here, since the life of books often exceeds the life of pesticides considered to be safe). Generally speaking, malathion sprays will control white flies.

New growth and flowers malformed. The effect of microscopic cyclamen mites. Spray or dip plant, using a miticide (available at garden-supply centers). Shell No-Pest Strips are also effective when placed in the same room with mite-infested plants. Cyclamen mite most often attacks cyclamen, African violets and any African violet relative known as a gesneriad, for example, columnea, episcia and gloxinia.

All growth weak, spindly, pale. Lack of light, lack of fertilizer, or both. Plants that are light-starved in an atmosphere that is too hot and too dry often display these symptoms.

Green insects clustered on new growth. A common symptom of outdoor container plants. Aphids are present. Mostly these are not difficult to control—in fact, in the outdoor garden they tend to go away in time whether or not you spray them. However, malathion will take care of them easily.

Silvery, blistered areas in leaves and on flower petals. Thrips are the cause, a tiny, threadlike, black insect that rasps away at tender plant tissue. Outdoors or indoors a spray or dip of malathion will eradicate thrips. Inside a Shell No-Pest Strip placed in the same room with infected plants will stop thrips.

Appendix A

Where to Buy
Plants, Supplies and Equipment

Abbey Garden, Box 30331, Santa Barbara, Calif. 93105—Complete listing of cacti and other succulents; catalog 25¢.

Abbot's Nursery, Route 4, Box 482, Mobile, Ala. 36609—Camellias.

Aladdin Industries, Inc., Nashville, Tenn. 37210—Manufacturers of growth chambers and fluorescent-light gardening equipment.

Alberts & Merkel Bros., Inc., 2210 S. Federal Highway, Boynton Beach, Fla. 33435—Orchids, plus an amazing array of tropical foliage and flowering house plants; 25¢ for list.

Aluminum Greenhouses, Inc., 14615 Lorain Ave., Cleveland, Ohio 44111—Prefabricated home greenhouses.

Annalee Violetry, 29050 214th Place, Bayside, N.Y. 11360—African violets.

Antonelli Bros., 2545 Capitola Rd., Santa Cruz, Calif. 95060—Tuberous begonias, gloxinias, achimenes.

Louise Barnaby, 12178 Highview St., Vicksburg, Mich. 49097—African violets; send stamp for list.

Charles Bateman, Box 25, Thornhill, Ontario, Canada—Liquid whale organic fertilizer.

Mrs. Mary V. Boose, 9 Turney Place, Trumbull, Conn. 06611—African violets and episcias; 15¢ for list.

John Brudy's Rare Plant House, P.O. Box 1348, Cocoa Beach, Fla. 32931—Unusual seeds and plants.

Buell's Greenhouses, Weeks Road, Eastford, Conn. 06242—Complete listing of gloxinias, African violets and other gesneriads; send $1 for catalog.

Burgess Seed & Plant Co., 67 E. Battle Creek, Galesburg, Mich. 49053—Houseplants, vegetables, herbs, bulbs.

W. Atlee Burpee Co., 18th and Hunting Park Ave., Philadelphia, Pa. 19132—Seeds, bulbs, supplies and equipment for container gardening.

David Buttram, P.O. Box 193, Independence, Mo. 64051—African violets; send 10¢ for list.

Cactus Gem Nursery, 10092 Mann Dr., Cupertino, Calif. (visit Thurs.-Sun.); by mail write P.O. Box 327, Aromas, Calif. 95004.

Castle Violets, 614 Castle Rd., Colorado Springs, Colo. 80904—African violets.

Champion's African Violets, 8848 Van Hoesen Rd., Clay, N.Y. 13041—African violets; send stamp for list.

Victor Constantinov, 3321 21st St., Apt. 7, San Francisco, Calif. 94110—African violets, columneas and episcias; send stamp for list.

Cook's Geranium Nursery, 714 N. Grand, Lyons, Kans. 67544—Geraniums; send 25¢ for catalog.

Davis Cactus Garden, 1522 Jefferson St., Kerrville, Tex. 78028—Send 25¢ for catalog.

DeGiorgi Bros., Inc., Council Bluffs, Iowa —Seeds of all kinds for container gardens.

P. de Jager and Sons, 188 Asbury St., South Hamilton, Mass. 01982—Bulbs for indoors and outdoors.

L. Easterbrook Greenhouses, 10 Craig St., Butler, Ohio 44822—African violets, other gesneriads, terrarium plants and supplies. Complete catalog 75¢.

Electric Farm, 104 B Lee Rd., Oak Hill, N.Y. 12460—Gesneriads; send self-addressed stamped envelope for list.

Farmer Seed and Nursery Co., Faribault, Minn. 55021—Flowers, bulbs, vegetables, herbs, fruit for container gardens.

Fennell Orchid Co., Inc., 26715 S.W. 157th Ave., Homestead, Fla. 33030.

Fernwood Plants, 1311 Fernwood Pacific Dr., Topanga, Calif. 90290—Rare and unusual cacti.

Ffoulkes, 610 Bryan St., Jacksonville, Fla. 32202—African violets; send 25¢ for list.

Henry Field Seed & Nursery Co., 407 Sycamore, Shenandoah, Iowa 51601—Flowers, bulbs, vegetables, herbs, fruit for container gardens.

Fischer Greenhouses, Linwood, N.J. 08221—African violets and other gesneriads; send 20¢ for catalog.

Floralite Co., 4124 E. Oakwood Rd., Oak Creek, Wis. 53154—Fluorescent-light gardening equipment and supplies.

Fox Orchids, 6615 W. Markham, Little Rock, Ark. 72205—Orchids and supplies for growing them at home.

Arthur Freed Orchids, Inc., 5731 S. Bonsall Dr., Malibu, Calif. 90265—Orchids and supplies for growing them.

French, J. Howard, Baltimore Pike, Lima, Pa. 19060—Bulbs for forcing.

Girard Nurseries, P.O. Box 428, Geneva, Ohio 44041—Bonsai materials.

The Greenhouse, 9515 Flower St., Bellflower, Calif. 90706—Fluorescent-light gardening equipment.

Grigsby Cactus Gardens, 2354 Bella Vista Dr., Vista, Calif. 92083—Catalog 50¢.

Gurney Seed and Nursery Co., Yankton, S.Dak. 57078—Houseplants, flowers, vegetables, herbs, fruits for container gardens.

Orchids by Hausermann, Inc., P.O. Box 363, Elmhurst, Ill. 60126—Complete array of orchids and supplies for growing them.

Helen's Cactus, 2205 Mirasol, Browns-ville, Tex. 78520—Send stamp for list.

Henrietta's Nursery, 1345 N. Brawley Ave., Fresno, Calif. 93705—Cacti and other succulents; catalog 20¢.

Hilltop Farm, Route 3, Box 216, Cleveland, Tex.—Geraniums and herbs.

Sim T. Holmes, 100 Tustarawas Rd., Beaver, Pa. 15009—African violets, miniature and regular; all grown under fluorescent lights.

The House of Violets, 936 Garland St. S.W., Camden, Ark. 71701—Self-watering African violet planters.

House Plant Corner, Box 131, Oxford, Md. 21654—Supplies and equipment for growing houseplants; send 20¢ for catalog.

Spencer M. Howard Orchid Imports, 11802 Huston St., N. Hollywood, Calif. 91607—Species and unusual orchids; free list.

Gordon M. Hoyt Orchids, Seattle Heights, Wash. 98036—Complete listing of interesting orchids for the home grower.

Hydroponic Chemical Co., Copley, Ohio 44321—Special fertilizers for container gardening.

Margaret Ilgenfritz Orchids, Blossom Lane, P.O. Box 1114, Monroe, Mich. 48161—Catalog $1.

Indoor Gardening Supplies, P.O. Box 40551, Detroit, Mich. 48240—Fluorescent-light gardening equipment.

Jones and Scully, 2200 N.W. 33rd Ave., Miami, Fla. 33142—Remarkable catalog of orchids and supplies for growing them; $3.50 per copy.

Kartuz Greenhouses, 92 Chestnut St., Wilmington, Mass. 01887—Begonias, gesneriads, wide range of other plants for container gardening; catalog 25¢.

Wm. Kirch—Orchids, Ltd., 2630 Waiomao Rd., Honolulu, Hawaii 96816—Orchids.

Kirkpatrick's, 27785 De Anza St., Barstow, Calif. 92311—Cacti/succulents; send 10¢ for list.

Kolb's Greenhouses, 725 Belvidere Rd., Phillipsburg, N.J. 08865—African violets; send stamp for list.

J & D Lamps, 245 S. Broadway, Yonkers, N.Y. 10705—Fluorescent-light gardening equipment.

Lauray, Undermountain Rd., Rt. 41, Salisbury, Conn. 06068—Gesneriads, cacti/

succulents, begonias; send 50¢ for catalog.

Logee's Greenhouses, 55 North St., Danielson, Conn. 06239—Complete selection of rare and unusual plants for container gardening; catalog $1.

Lord and Burnham, Irvington, N.Y. 10533—Home greenhouses, window greenhouses.

Lyndon Lyon, 14 Mutchler St., Dolgeville, N.Y. 13329—African violets and other gesneriads.

Mary's African Violets, 19788 San Juan, Detroit, Mich. 48221—Supplies and lighting equipment.

Earl May Seed & Nursery Co., Shenandoah, Iowa 51603—Flowers, vegetables, herbs, trees, shrubs, fruit to grow in containers.

Rod McLellan Co., 1450 El Camino Real, S. San Francisco, Calif. 94080—Orchids and supplies for growing them at home.

Merry Gardens, Camden, Maine 04843—Houseplants, herbs, unusual plants for container gardens; catalog $1.

Mini-Roses, P.O. Box 245, Station A., Dallas, Tex. 75208—Miniature roses for container gardens.

Modlin's Cactus Gardens, Rt. 4, Box 3035, Vista, Calif. 92083—Catalog 25¢

Cactus by Mueller, 10411 Rosedale Highway, Bakersfield, Calif. 93308—10¢ stamp for list.

Nature's Way Products, 3505 Mozart Ave., Cincinnati, Ohio 45211—Perlite, other soil conditioners, fertilizer, potting soils; send stamp for list.

J. A. Nearing Co., 10788 Tucker St., Beltsville, Md. 20705—Prefabricated home greenhouses.

Nichols Garden Nursery, 1190 N. Pacific Highway, Albany, Ore. 97321—Unusual vegetables; herbs.

Walter F. Nicke, Hudson, N.Y. 12534—Useful as well as unusual gardening supplies and equipment, much of it made in England.

Norvell Greenhouses, 318 S. Greenacres Rd., Greenacres, Wash. 99016—Houseplants.

George W. Park Seed Co., Inc., Greenwood, S.C. 29646—Seeds, bulbs, fluorescent-light gardening supplies and equipment; very large, complete catalog, free for the asking.

Penn Valley Orchids, 239 Old Gulph Rd., Wynnewood, Pa. 19096—Orchids.

Robert B. Peters Co., Inc., 2833 Pennsylvania St., Allentown, Pa.—Peters fertilizers, available in several formulations designed for specific growth responses.

Ra-Pid-Gro Corp., 88 Ossian, Dansville, N.Y. 14437—Manufacturers of Ra-Pid-Gro, root and foliar fertilizer.

Redfern's Prefab Greenhouses, 55 Mt. Hermon Rd., Scotts Valley, Calif. 95060.

Redwood Domes, 2664 Highway 1, Aptos, Calif. 95003 — Prefabricated home greenhouses.

Schmelling's African Violets, 5133 Peck Hill Rd., Jamesville, N.Y. 13078—African violets; catalog 20¢.

Schultz Co., 11730 Northline, St. Louis, Mo. 63043—Manufacturers of excellent container garden fertilizer.

Sequoia Nursery, 2519 E. Noble, Visalia, Calif. 93277—Miniature roses.

Shaffer's Tropical Gardens, Inc., 1220 41st Ave., Capitola, Calif. 95010—Orchids.

P. R. Sharp, 104 N. Chapel Ave., #3, Alhambra, Calif. 91801—South American and Mexican cacti.

Shoplite Co., Inc., 566 Franklin Ave., Nutley, N.J. 07110—Fluorescent-light gardening equipment; catalog 25¢.

R. H. Shumway Seedsman, Rockford, Ill. 61101 — Flowers, vegetables, herbs, bulbs, fruit, trees, shrubs for container gardening.

Singers' Growing Things, 6385 Enfield Ave., Reseda, Calif. 91335—Succulents for container gardens.

Smith's Cactus Garden, P.O. Box 871, Paramount, Calif. 90723—Send 30¢ for list.

Star Roses, Box 203, West Grove, Pa. 19390—Miniature roses, other woody plants for container gardening.

Fred A. Stewart, Inc., Orchids, 1212 E. Las Tunas Dr., San Gabriel, Calif. 91778—Orchids.

Ed Storms, 4223 Pershing, Ft. Worth, Tex. 76107—Lithops and other succulents.

Sturdi Built Manufacturing Co., 11304 S. W. Boones Ferry Rd., Portland, Ore. —Prefabricated home greenhouses.

Sunnybrook Farms, 9448 Mayfield Rd., Chesterland, Ohio 44026 — Herbs; scented geraniums; source for *Aloe vera,* the "unguentine plant."

Texas Greenhouse Co., Inc., 2717 St. Louis Ave., Ft. Worth, Tex. 76110— Prefabricated home greenhouses.

Thompson & Morgan, Ltd., P.O. Box 24, Somerdale, N.J. 08083—Many unusual seeds of plants for container gardens.

Three Springs Fisheries, Lilypons, Md. 21717—Aquarium plants.

Tinari Greenhouses, Box 190, 2325 Valley Rd., Huntingdon Valley, Pa. 19006 —African violets, gesneriads, supplies and equipment; catalog 25¢.

William Tricker, Inc., Allendale Ave., Saddle River, N.J. 07458 — Aquarium plants.

Tube Craft, Inc., 1311 W. 80th St., Cleveland, Ohio 44102—Fluorescent-light gardening equipment.

Turner Greenhouses, P.O. Box 1260, Goldsboro, N.C. 27530—Prefabricated home greenhouses.

Van Ness Water Gardens, 2460 N. Euclid Ave., Upland, Calif. 91786—Aquarium plants.

Volkmann Bros. Greenhouses, 2714 Minert St., Dallas, Tex. 75219—Send stamped, self-addressed long envelope for catalog of African violets and supplies, including the Reservoir Wick Pot.

Wilson Brothers, Roachdale, Ind. 47121 —Geraniums, begonias, many other flowering plants for container gardens.

H. E. Wise, 3710 June St., San Bernardino, Calif. 92405—Cacti; send stamp for list.

Mrs. Ernie Wurster, Route 1 Box 156, Elizabeth, Ill. 61028—African violets; send 15¢ for list.

Appendix B

Plant Societies and Periodicals

African Violet Magazine, bimonthly publication of the African Violet Society of America, Inc., Box 1326, Knoxville, Tenn. 37901.

American Fern Journal, quarterly publication of the American Fern Society, Biological Sciences Group, University of Connecticut, Storrs, Conn. 06268.

American Horticulturist, bimonthly publication of the American Horticultural Society, Mount Vernon, Va. 22121.

American Ivy Society Bulletin, periodical of the American Ivy Society, 128 W. 58th St., New York, N.Y. 10019.

American Orchid Society Bulletin, monthly publication of the American Orchid Society, Inc., Botanical Museum of Harvard University, Cambridge, Mass. 02138.

The Begonian, monthly of the American Begonia Society, Inc., 139 N. Ledoux Rd., Beverly Hills, Calif. 90211.

Bonsai (quarterly) and *ABStracts* (monthly newsletter), publications of the American Bonsai Society, 953 S. Shore Dr., Lake Waukomis, Parkville, Mo. 64151.

Bonsai Magazine, ten times a year, publication of Bonsai Clubs International, 445 Blake St., Menlo Park, Calif. 94025.

The Bromeliad Journal, bimonthly publication of the Bromeliad Society, Inc., P.O. Box 3279, Santa Monica, Calif. 90403.

Cactus and Succulent Journal, bimonthly publication of the Cactus and Succulent Society of America, Inc., Box 167, Reseda, Calif. 91335.

The Camellia Journal, quarterly publication of the American Camellia Society, Box 212, Fort Valley, Ga. 31030.

Cymbidium Society News, monthly publication of the Cymbidium Society of America, Inc., 6787 Worsham Dr., Whittier, Calif. 90602.

Epiphyllum Bulletin, publication of the

Epiphyllum Society of America, Inc., 218 E. Greystone Ave., Monrovia, Calif. 91016.

Geraniums Around the World, quarterly publication of the International Geranium Society, 11960 Pascal Ave., Colton, Calif. 92324.

Gesneriad Saintpaulia News, bimonthly publication of the American Gesneria Society, 11983 Darlington Ave., Los Angeles, Calif. 90049.

Gesneriad Saintpaulia News, bimonthly publication of Saintpaulia International, P.O. Box 10604, Knoxville, Tenn. 37919.

The Gloxinian, bimonthly publication of the American Gloxinia/Gesneriad Society, Inc., P.O. Box 174, New Milford, Conn. 06776.

Light Garden, bimonthly publication of the Indoor Light Gardening Society of America, Inc., 128 W. 58th St., New York, N.Y. 10019.

Monthly Fern Lessons, with newsletter and annual magazine, publications of the Los Angeles International Fern Society, 2423 Burritt Ave., Redondo Beach, Calif. 90278.

The National Fuchsia Fan, monthly publication of the National Fuchsia Society, 10934 E. Flory St., Whittier, Calif. 90606.

The Orchid Digest, 25 Ash Ave., Corte Madera, Calif. 94925.

Plantlife-Amaryllis Yearbook, bulletin of the American Plant Life Society, Box 150, La Jolla, Calif. 92037.

Plants Alive, monthly magazine about indoor gardening, 2100 N. 45th, Seattle, Wash. 98103.

Princepes, quarterly publication of the Palm Society, 1320 S. Venetian Way, Miami, Fla. 33139.

Seed Pod, quarterly publication of the American Hibiscus Society, Box 98, Eagle Lake, Fla. 33139.

Terrarium Topics, published by The Terrarium Association, 57 Wolfpit Ave., Norwalk, Conn. 06851.

Under Glass, bimonthly devoted to home greenhouse growing; c/o Lord and Burnham, Irvington, N.Y. 10533.

Index